The Institute of Chartered Accountants in England and Wales

LAW

For exams in 2018

Question Bank

www.icaew.com

Law
The Institute of Chartered Accountants in England and Wales

ISBN: 978-1-78363-881-9
Previous ISBN: 978-1-78363-457-6

First edition 2007
Eleventh edition 2017

The content of this publication is intended to prepare students for the ICAEW examinations, and should not be used as professional advice.

British Library Cataloguing-in-Publication Data
A catalogue record for this book is available from the British Library

Originally printed in the United Kingdom on paper obtained from traceable, sustainable sources.

Contents

The following questions are exam standard. Unless told otherwise, these questions are the style, content and format that you can expect in your exam.

Exam

This assessment will consist of 50 questions with equal marks, adding up to 100 marks.

The questions are of the following types:

- **Multiple choice** – select 1 from 4 options A, B, C or D (see Chapter 1 Q3)

- **Multi-part multiple choice** – select 1 from 2, 3 or 4 options, for two or more question parts (see Chapter 1 Q7)

In this question bank you should select only one option per question unless told otherwise.

The assessment is 1.5 hours long and at least 55 marks are required to pass this assessment.

Our website has the latest information, guidance and exclusive resources to help you prepare for this assessment. Find everything you need, from exam webinars, sample assessments, errata sheets and the syllabus to advice from the examiners at icaew.com/exams if you're studying the ACA and icaew.com/cfabstudents if you're studying ICAEW CFAB.

Question Bank

Chapter 1: Contract formation

1 Which of the following types of contract must be in writing or evidenced in writing?

    A   A partnership agreement

    B   A contract for the sale of goods

    C   An agreement for the transfer of land

    D   An employment contract   LO 1a

2 Are the following statements true or false?

A statute cannot override terms of a contract that have been expressly agreed between the parties.

    A   True

    B   False

All persons over 18 have capacity to enter into any contract.

    C   True

    D   False   LO 1a

3 Which of the following terms describes a contract where one party may set it aside, but property transferred before avoidance is usually irrecoverable from a third party?

    A   Void

    B   Voidable

    C   Unenforceable

    D   Valid   LO 1a

4 A commercial contract for the sale of land, which is based on an agreement and is supported by consideration but which is not made in the correct form, is:

    A   void

    B   voidable

    C   unenforceable

    D   illegal   LO 1a

5   Gary intends to promise Carl that he (Gary) will pay the debts owed to Carl by Duncan, in the event that Duncan fails to pay them himself. Which of the following is true with regard to Gary's proposed guarantee so that it will be enforceable in a court of law?

A   It must be by deed

B   It must be in writing

C   It can be oral provided it is evidenced in writing

D   It can be oral only   LO 1a

6   Denzil puts a notice in the local post office saying 'Reward. Lost cavalier King Charles spaniel named Barnie. £150 reward for his safe return'. Florence finds Barnie and, unaware of Denzil's notice, takes him to Denzil's home address which is inscribed on the dog's name tag. Which of the following statements best describes the legal position?

A   Florence is not entitled to the reward. The offer is invalid as it is not made to an identifiable class of persons

B   Florence is entitled to the reward. The offer is valid and her acceptance of the offer can be inferred from her act of returning the dog

C   Florence is not entitled to the reward. She failed to claim the reward at the time of returning Barnie (and accepting Denzil's offer) and has therefore waived her right to receive it

D   Florence is not entitled to the reward as she did not even know that a reward was being offered

                                                                                                       LO 1a

7   Clarence sells champagne and high quality wines from home. He delivers a glossy flyer to all the £1m plus homes in the Clifton area of Bristol, offering a 1998 Chablis for £30 a bottle. On reading his copy of the flyer, Kenton goes to Clarence's home and asks for a case of Chablis.

     Is the flyer issued by Clarence a valid offer?

A   Yes

B   No

     Is Clarence in breach of contract if he says to Kenton that the Chablis is out of stock and that he is unable to get hold of any more?

C   Yes

D   No   LO 1a

8   Matilda goes shopping in her local village store. Roses are on display priced at £2 each. Matilda has £6 in her purse and takes three roses to the counter to pay.

     Does the display of clearly-priced roses constitute an offer which Matilda accepts when she picks up the roses?

A   Yes

B   No

     Can the shopkeeper refuse to sell the roses to Matilda?

C   Yes

D   No   LO 1a

9 A local newspaper advertises '50 Whizzalong scooters remaining. 3 feet high. Only £20 each.' Which legal term best describes the advert?

    A   Offer

    B   Statement of intention

    C   Invitation to treat

    D   Supply of information   LO 1a

---

10 Which of the following will **not** have the effect of terminating an offer?

    A   Rejection

    B   Counter offer

    C   When a pre-condition is satisfied

    D   A lapse of time   LO 1a

---

11 Michael offers to sell his Laser 2000 sailing dinghy to Rupert for £1,500, provided he gets the job for which he has just been interviewed, since that would result in him having to live somewhere too far from sailing facilities. Rupert is delighted and thinks £1,500 is an excellent price. Michael fails to get the job. What is the consequence of Michael failing to get the job?

    A   The offer is terminated

    B   The contract is rendered voidable

    C   The contract is rendered unconditional

    D   The contract is rendered unenforceable   LO 1a

---

12 On Monday, George offers to sell his piano to Hilda for £1,500, to be delivered on Thursday. On Tuesday, Hilda replies, saying that she will only buy the piano if George will delay delivery until the following Monday. George doesn't reply but sells his piano to Ivy on Thursday. On Friday, Hilda sees George and accepts his offer. Is there a binding contract between George and Hilda?

    A   Yes, Hilda's reply on Tuesday constitutes an acceptance of the offer

    B   No, Hilda's reply on Tuesday constitutes a counter offer which destroys the original offer

    C   No, the offer is terminated when George sells the piano to Ivy on Thursday

    D   Yes, Hilda's reply on Tuesday is a request for information only and on Friday she accepts his offer   LO 1a

---

13 Frank offered Mary his lawnmower for £200. Mary asked whether he might be willing to accept £100 now and £100 at the end of the month when she is paid. Which of the following best describes the status of Mary's reply?

    A   It is a rejection of Frank's offer

    B   It is an implied acceptance because she was clearly agreeable to the price

    C   It is a counter offer

    D   It is a request for information   LO 1a

---

14 Mark e-mails Nathan and offers to sell his tandem to him for £250. Nathan texts him back to say that he'd love it but he will only pay £230. Two days later Mark says he'll accept £230 but Nathan has bought one on eBay for £200. Which of the following best describes the legal position between the parties?

A   Nathan's reply is a rejection of Mark's offer

B   Nathan's reply is a counter offer which Mark accepts

C   Nathan's reply is merely a request for information as to whether Mark will accept £20 less

D   Nathan's reply constitutes a counter offer but this is revoked when he buys a tandem from eBay

LO 1a

15 Are the following statements true or false?

If an offer states that it will remain open for three months, the offeror cannot revoke it before three months have passed.

A   True

B   False

A letter of revocation is effective when posted.

C   True

D   False

LO 1a

16 Ralph writes to Theo offering to buy Theo's sand yacht for £300. In his letter, he writes 'If I do not hear from you, I shall consider it mine and pick it up on Tuesday.' Which of the following best describes the legal position as to whether or not a contract exists?

A   There is a contract because Ralph waived the need for acceptance

B   There is a contract because Theo complied with Ralph's terms exactly

C   There is a contract because acceptance can be inferred from Theo's conduct

D   There is no contract because there is no positive act to indicate acceptance

LO 1a

17 On 28 May, Abigail writes to Gill and offers to sell her all her old accountancy study manuals for £50. Gill posts a letter together with a cheque for £50 on 1 June saying that she'll pick them up on 3 June. However on 2 June, Abigail discovers that she has failed two of her papers and so sends a letter to Gill saying that the books are no longer for sale. On 3 June, each receives the other's letter.

Does the letter of revocation take effect on 2 June?

A   Yes

B   No

Does Gill's acceptance take effect on 3 June?

C   Yes

D   No

LO 1a

18 Are the following statements true or false?

Acceptance may be express or inferred from conduct.

A   True

B   False

Acceptance must always be communicated to the offeror in order for it to be effective.

C   True

D   False   LO 1a

19 On Monday, Peter writes to Quentin offering to sell his car to Quentin for £900. Peter's letter is received the next day. On Wednesday, Peter posts a letter to Quentin saying that he has changed his mind. Later that day, Quentin speaks to Peter and says that he accepts his offer. Is there a valid contract between Peter and Quentin?

A   No, because Peter posted his revocation before Quentin accepted the offer

B   Yes, because Quentin accepts the offer before he receives Peter's letter of revocation

C   No, because Quentin's acceptance should have been in writing since the offer was made in writing

D   Yes, because Quentin's acceptance is made in a more expeditious manner than the offer
                                                                                                           LO 1a

20 Are the following statements true or false?

An acceptance of a contractual offer sent by email takes effect as soon as the person accepting the offer presses the 'send' key.

A   True

B   False

Whether or not postal acceptance is within the contemplation of the parties is a question of fact and may be deduced from all the circumstances.

C   True

D   False   LO 1a

21 Are the following statements true or false?

Where the offeror prescribes a mode of communication of acceptance, the offeree can normally use an alternative mode, provided it is at least as expeditious as the mode prescribed.

A   True

B   False

Where no mode of communication of acceptance is prescribed, the offeree should use the same mode as that used for the offer.

C   True

D   False   LO 1a

22 On 1 May, Hugh offered to sell his boat to Jeff for £5,000, stating that his offer had to be accepted by notice in writing. Jeff posted a letter of acceptance on 3 May, but it never arrived.

Does the postal rule apply ie, is the acceptance effective as soon as it is posted?

A   Yes

B   No

Is there a contract between Hugh and Jeff?

C   Yes

D   No   LO 1a

---

23 Brenda writes to Carol on 1 January offering to sell her gold necklace for £100. Carol receives the letter on 3 January and on 5 January posts a letter accepting Brenda's offer and sends a cheque for £100. In the meantime, however, Brenda has sold the necklace to her sister Daisy for £150 believing that Carol wasn't interested. She wrote to Carol telling her this on 4 January but the letter wasn't received by Carol until 6 January. Brenda received Carol's cheque on 7 January. Which of the following is true?

A   Carol's acceptance is effective on 5 January

B   Brenda's offer is revoked on 4 January

C   Carol's acceptance is effective on 7 January

D   There is no binding agreement between Brenda and Carol   LO 1a

---

24 With regard to the terms of a contract, answer the following:

Where a contract is in writing, will the courts allow the parties to rely on any terms that are agreed between them but not embodied in the written document?

A   Yes

B   No

Can a term implied by custom and practice be overridden by a written term?

C   Yes

D   No   LO 1a

---

25 Mr and Mrs Higgins own two flats in Bristol which they let to students. When their eldest son, Crispin, was offered a place at Bristol University to read Law, he and his parents entered into a tenancy agreement allowing him to reside at one of the flats during his university studies for a rent of £190 per month. He was allowed to sublet the second bedroom for a rent of £200 per month. In the light of the rebuttable presumption that no intention to create legal relations exists in the case of a family, social or domestic arrangement, which of the following statements best describes the legal position as to whether the necessary intention to create legal relations exists in this instance?

A   No, because it is a family or domestic arrangement and so no such intention is presumed

B   No, because the fact that Crispin pays a reduced rent is evidence that no such intention exists

C   Yes, the normal presumption in family arrangements is rebutted by the fact that the parties enter into a written agreement and rent is payable

D   Yes, because the normal presumption does not apply where the arrangement relates to property   LO 1a

26 Are the following statements true or false?

There is a rebuttable presumption that social, domestic and family arrangements are not intended to be legally binding.

A   True

B   False

There is an irrebuttable presumption that parties to a commercial agreement intend it to be legally binding.

C   True

D   False   LO 1a

27 Which of the following statements best describes consideration?

A   Consideration must be adequate and sufficient

B   Consideration must be adequate but need not be sufficient

C   Consideration must be sufficient but need not be adequate

D   Consideration need be neither sufficient nor adequate   LO 1a

28 Can the following constitute valid consideration?

The payment of £1 per year as rent for a house

A   Yes

B   No

A promise by Adam not to pursue his action for breach of contract against Ben, if Ben agrees to do Adam's accounts for him for 12 months without charge

C   Yes

D   No   LO 1a

29 Zoe was employed to give one lunchtime recital per month at a prestigious eating venue in London. Her contract contained a provision that she would stay behind and meet with appreciative members of the audience after the recital, as part of the venue's aim of making music more accessible and less elitist. After about 18 months, Zoe's recitals had become very popular but she was always keen to get away quickly after each performance. The manager offered her £50 (on top of her recital fee) if she would stay behind and meet with appreciative members of the audience for up to an hour after each recital. Can Zoe enforce the promise to pay her the extra £50?

    A   Yes. It is a fresh promise that the manager chose to make

    B   Yes, because the contractual provision had become redundant through its non-observance

    C   No, because she was obliged to perform that duty anyway

    D   No. It was simply a goodwill gesture and is not intended to be legally binding   LO 1a

30 Zak owes Eve £100. Finding that he has insufficient cash, Zak offers Eve his bicycle worth £90 instead. Eve accepts. Which of the following statements best describes the legal position as to whether there is valid consideration?

    A   Yes, Eve was not already entitled to the bicycle so it is sufficient consideration for waiver of the debt

    B   No, the bicycle is not sufficient as it does not match or exceed the value of the debt

    C   No, consideration must be in money or money's worth

    D   Yes, a bicycle constitutes sufficient consideration because it has an identifiable value   LO 1a

31 In which of the following scenarios is there **insufficient** consideration for a waiver of rights by Oscar where Humphrey owes him £1,000 to be paid on 13 May?

    A   Oscar agrees to accept a car instead

    B   Oscar agrees to accept £980 on 13 May in cash

    C   Oscar agrees to accept £980 from Humphrey's sister in full satisfaction of the debt

    D   Humphrey agrees to pay Oscar £700 on 1 May   LO 1a

32 With regard to terms being implied into contracts, are the following true or false?

    The courts will imply a term into a contract if required to do so by statute.

    A   True

    B   False

    Terms may be implied on the basis of a custom or practice of a particular trade.

    C   True

    B   False   LO 1a

33 Prunella agrees to pay Paul £500 if Paul will landscape Phillip's garden. There is no agency relationship and the Contract (Rights of Third Parties) Act 1999 does not apply. Who may enforce the terms of the contract?

   A   Prunella, Paul and Phillip

   B   Prunella and Phillip only

   C   Paul and Phillip only

   D   Prunella and Paul only   LO 1a

34 Which of the following requirements need to be satisfied for a third party to seek to enforce a contractual term under the Contracts (Rights of Third Parties) Act 1999?

   A   That the contract expressly so provides

   B   That the third party must exist at the time the contract is made but need not be known to the parties

   C   That the third party must be identified in some way in the contract

   D   That the term to be enforced by the third party contains only positive rights   LO 1a

35 In relation to the intention to create legal relations:

   The parties to a social or domestic agreement are presumed to have intended the agreement to be legally enforceable, although this intention is rebuttable.

   A   True

   B   False

   The parties to a commercial agreement are presumed to have intended the arrangement to be legally enforceable.

   C   True

   D   False   Sample Paper LO 1a

36 On Monday, Andrew advertised his car for sale for £5,000 in a local newspaper. Brian saw the advertisement and telephoned Andrew offering him £4,500 for the car. Andrew eventually offered to sell the car to Brian for £4,800. Brian replied that he would need to test-drive the car before he could agree such a price. Brian then agreed a time to meet at Andrew's house the following weekend for the test-drive.

   On Friday, Andrew sold his car to his neighbour Carol for £4,500.

   Are the following statements true or false?

   Andrew's advertisement in the newspaper is purely an invitation to treat and as such is incapable of acceptance and forming a legally binding contract.

   A   True

   B   False

   Brian has no right of action against Andrew because no acceptance took place.

   C   True

   D   False   Sample Paper LO 1a

37 Matt runs a small hotel. One of his friends, Louise, decorated two of the bedrooms for him, as a surprise, when he was away on holiday. On his return, Matt was delighted and agreed to give her a laptop in consideration for all her work. As a separate matter, he also agreed to pay Louise's brother, Adam, the sum of £300 to fit new lights and sockets in the bedrooms. Adam performs the work.

When Louise and Adam come to collect the laptop and the money Matt refuses to give them either.

Which of the following statements is correct?

A The contract with Louise is valid; the contract with Adam is valid

B The contract with Louise is valid; the contract with Adam is invalid

C The contract with Louise is invalid; the contract with Adam is invalid

D The contract with Louise is invalid; the contract with Adam is valid   Sample Paper LO 1a

38 On 1 February, Harry posts a letter to Beth offering to sell his car. On 2 February, Beth receives Harry's letter.

On 3 February, Harry changes his mind and posts a letter to Beth telling her that the car is no longer for sale. On the same day, Beth posts a letter to Harry accepting the offer contained in his letter of 1 February.

On 4 February, Beth receives Harry's letter informing her that the car is no longer for sale.

Is there a valid contract between Beth and Harry regarding the sale of Harry's car?

A Yes, acceptance took place on 3 February and Harry's revocation took place on 4 February

B No, Harry revoked the offer before Beth posted her acceptance

C Yes, Harry cannot revoke the offer once it has been communicated to Beth

D No, Harry's revocation took place on 3 February so Beth's acceptance is too late

Sample Paper LO 1a

39 A contractual offer may be terminated by:

Rejection

A Yes

B No

Lapse of time

C Yes

D No   Sample Paper LO 1a

40 Arthur agrees to carry out a major building project for Bashir. He commences the works before the contract between the parties is executed, because their solicitors are still finalising some of its terms. After two weeks, Bashir has decided that he is not at all happy with the work so far completed by Arthur and plans to sue him for breach of contract. Which of the following best describes the legal position?

A   Bashir must sue in tort because there is no contract between them

B   The terms of the contract will be those which have been agreed so far

C   The parties must finalise the contract before either party may sue the other for breach

D   A contract is likely to be deemed to exist and its terms will be a question of fact in all the circumstances

LO 1a

Law: Question Bank

1   Which term best describes a contract, such as a building contract, that provides for payment at various stages of the contractor's progress?

   A   A divided contract

   B   A segmented contract

   C   A severable contract

   D   A partial contract   LO 1b

2   Anna employs Derek to build a children's playground in the grounds of her house. Derek finishes the work on time but omits to paint one side of the mega-slide frame. Which of the following best describes the legal position?

   A   Anna is not obliged to pay Derek until he completes the job exactly as required

   B   Derek is entitled to full payment under the doctrine of substantial performance

   C   Derek is entitled to payment of the contract price less a reasonable amount in respect of the omission made

   D   Anna should seek an order of specific performance to ensure that the contract is completed
                                                                                                            LO 1b

3   Abigail agrees to let her flat to Xavier for one day for the purpose of viewing a carnival. Xavier pays her a £50 deposit with £80 due to be paid at the end of the carnival. Due to civil unrest, the government prohibits all street entertainment and the carnival is cancelled just before Xavier is due to travel to the flat. Neither party has incurred any costs (save for payment of the deposit) in performance of the contract. Applying the Law Reform (Frustrated Contracts) Act 1943, which of the following statements is correct?

   A   Abigail can keep the deposit but cannot claim the balance

   B   Abigail can keep the deposit and Xavier is liable to pay the balance

   C   Abigail must pay back the deposit and Xavier need not pay the balance

   D   Abigail can keep the deposit and Xavier must pay an additional £15 so that each party bears an equal loss   Sample Paper LO 1b

4   Are the following statements true or false under the Law Reform (Frustrated Contracts) Act 1943?

Where a contract has been frustrated and B has derived no benefit from it, A may nonetheless retain a part of any deposit paid by B, in order to cover the cost of any expenses incurred in performance of the contract up to the time the contract was frustrated.

A   True

B   False

If either party has obtained a valuable benefit (other than the payment of money) under the contract before it is discharged by frustration, the court has a discretion to order that party to pay all or part of that value.

C   True

D   False   LO 1b

---

5   Are the following statements true or false?

Anticipatory breach may be implied from conduct and need not be explicit.

A   True

B   False

Where an innocent party elects to treat a contract as discharged, they waive the right to claim damages from the party in default.

C   True

D   False   LO 1b

---

6   Monster Mowers Ltd agrees to sell one of its ride-on mowers to Geoff in the knowledge that Geoff is taking on new customers from Percy, a commercial gardener, who is retiring and that Geoff is unable to cope with the increased workload with his present mower. The company fails to deliver the mower until 10 days after the due date for delivery and Geoff is forced to continue working with his old mower as best he can. As a result he is unable to complete all the contracts he has agreed with Percy's old customers. He is also unable to accept an offer from the local botanical gardens to be their grass-cutting contractor for the next 12 months because he cannot begin work immediately. Which of the following statements best describes the legal position of Monster Mowers Ltd?

A   The company would be entitled to assume that Geoff could perform his contracts without the new mower and will not be liable for damages as a result

B   The company will be liable for damages in respect of breaches of Geoff's contracts with existing customers but not the new customers from Percy's business

C   The company will be liable for damages in respect of breaches of Geoff's contracts with all his customers but not in respect of the botanical gardens' potential contract as this was not a normal loss and the company was not aware of it

D   The company will be liable for damages in respect of breaches of contract with all his customers and for the lost contract with the botanical gardens since this was a reasonably foreseeable part of Geoff's business plans with his new mower   LO 1b

7   Are the following statements true or false?

Damages for breach of contract are primarily intended to restore the injured party to the same position they were in at the time when the contract was made.

A   True

B   False

The claimant is required to take every opportunity to mitigate their loss arising as a consequence of a breach of contract.

C   True

D   False   LO 1b

8   Henry agreed to advertise the services provided by his father's business, The Complete Service Ltd, in appropriate publications over a period of 24 months. It was agreed that Henry would be liable to pay a sum of £5,000 in respect of any advertising error or missed deadline. Which of the following describes this contractual provision?

A   A liquidated damages clause

B   An unliquidated damages clause

C   An exclusion clause

D   A penalty clause   LO 1b

9   James contracted to buy a rare sports car from Jeremy for £23,000 but refused to take delivery as agreed. Jeremy, who had recently bought the car for £20,000, was able to sell the car to Richard for £24,100, but sued James for breach of their contract. Which of the following best describes the legal position?

A   Jeremy is entitled to recover £23,000 from James, that being the agreed contract price and there being no excuse for James' breach

B   Jeremy is entitled to nominal damages only since he has been able to sell the car for greater profit

C   Jeremy is entitled only to recover from James the £20,000 that he had in fact paid for the car himself since he was able to sell the car on for profit following the breach by James

D   James is no longer in breach of contract because Jeremy has mitigated his loss totally   LO 1b

10   Siegfried employs Marij to plan and build a Go-Kart course on his field which he intends to open to the public on 1 May. His viability and market research studies lead him to expect that he will earn £300 per day in the first three months of business. Marij contracts to construct the course and surrounding areas according to certain plans and specifications and to complete the work by no later than 30 March for a contract price of £10,000. The contract provides that Marij will be liable to pay Siegfried £150 for every day work overruns the scheduled completion date. Which of the following best describes the legal position?

A   The provision is for unliquidated damages and is valid because it is less than the anticipated loss

B   The provision is for liquidated damages and is valid because the figure is not penal in nature and protects Siegfried's legitimate interest

C   The provision is void because it states a sum in excess of 1% of the total contract price

D   The provision is likely to be void because the same amount is payable regardless of the actual loss
LO 1b

11   Which of the following statements in relation to contractual remedies is incorrect?

A   Specific performance is awarded at the discretion of the court where damages would not be an adequate remedy

B   Specific performance is likely to be more appropriate than damages in a contract involving personal services

C   Specific performance is likely to be awarded in a contract for the sale of land

D   A mandatory injunction often has the same result as specific performance but is less common
LO 1b

12   Colin was engaged as a coach of the South of England Athletics Squad (SEAS) and his contract contained a clause that he would not coach any other team without the consent of the SEAS. The SEAS management discovered that unknown to them, he had in fact been coaching the South Wales team for three months and brought action against him for breach of contract. Which of the following is the most likely remedy to be granted in addition to possible damages?

A   A mandatory injunction

B   A *quantum meruit* award

C   Specific performance

D   A prohibitory injunction
LO 1b

13 The Unfair Contract Terms Act 1977 renders some exclusions void and others subject to the reasonableness test:

In a contract between two businesses, is a clause which limits liability for losses due to negligence void, however reasonable it might appear?

A   Yes

B   No

Is a clause limiting liability for personal injury resulting from negligence in a contract between two private individuals subject to the reasonableness test?

C   Yes

D   No   LO 1b

14 Which of the following descriptions best describes the statutory test of reasonableness under the Unfair Contract Terms Act 1977?

A   Whether an ordinary person in the normal course of business would consider the clause to be reasonable in all the circumstances

B   Whether it is fair and reasonable, with regard to all the circumstances which were, or which ought to have been known to the parties when the contract was made

C   Whether it is fair and reasonable with regard to all the circumstances which were known to or in the reasonable contemplation of the parties

D   Whether it is fair and reasonable to exclude liability, having regard to the relative bargaining strengths of the parties   LO 1b

15 Foul Foods Ltd, a company specialising in the production and sale of cream cakes on an industrial scale, bought a large oven from Ovens & Co intending to extend their existing business to include the production of pizza bases. The delivery of the oven was three months later than the contract date. During those three months Foul Foods Ltd tried unsuccessfully to buy another oven. Foul Foods Ltd has claimed for its lost profits in the following two ways:

(1) Profits which would have been made from the expected increase in business following their increased capacity; and

(2) Profits which they would have made from a lucrative contract for the supply of pizza bases to a nationwide supermarket chain for which they would have been able to bid.

Is Foul Foods Ltd's claim for its lost profits likely to be successful?

A   Yes, but only the lost profits from the expected general increase in trade are recoverable, not those from the loss of the lucrative supermarket contract

B   No, in accordance with the rules governing the award of damages for breach of contract both losses are too remote

C   Yes, the lost profits from the expected general increase in trade and the loss of the lucrative supermarket contract are recoverable

D   No, as Foul Foods Ltd have failed to mitigate their losses   Sample Paper LO 1b

16 The equitable remedy of specific performance can be awarded in cases involving:

The performance of personal services

A   True

B   False

A contract to build a house

C   True

D   False   Sample Paper LO 1b

---

17 Which of the following may be used to resolve disputes, even after court proceedings have been commenced?

(1) Negotiation
(2) Expert determination
(3) Mediation
(4) Adjudication

A   (1) only

B   (2), (3) and (4) only

C   (1) and (4) only

D   All of them   LO 1b

Chapter 3: Agency

1   Which of the following statements in relation to a contract made by an agent acting within their authority is incorrect?

    A   The principal can sue on the contract

    B   The third party can sue on the contract

    C   The agent can be sued on the contract

    D   The principal can be sued on the contract   LO 1c, 1e

2   Are the following statements true or false?

When an agent contracts with a third party, the principal must have capacity but the agent does not need to have capacity to enter into the contract.

    A   True

    B   False

An agency appointment must be made in writing.

    C   True

    D   False   LO 1c

3   Arthur worked for Lady Grey and part of his job was to buy plants, ornaments and furniture for the gardens of her country manor house. When her son, Harry, was due to retire from the services, she advised Arthur that Harry would be taking on his responsibilities. A few weeks later, Arthur ordered some very expensive roses and marble statues from Lady Grey's main supplier and collected the goods the next day for his own garden. The invoice was delivered to Lady Grey.

Is there an agency relationship between Arthur and Lady Grey in respect of the contract for the roses and statues?

    A   Yes

    B   No

Is Lady Grey bound to settle the invoice?

    C   Yes

    D   No   LO 1c

4   Stephen lives near an isolated headland in Cornwall. One day, he sees a Rolls Royce parked on the beach. No one is in sight but the tide is coming in rapidly. Stephen calls his neighbour and arranges for him to come and tow the Rolls Royce up the beach to safety. The neighbour is happy to oblige but wants payment for what he has done. When the owner, Anthony, returns, he refuses to pay because he says the action was not necessary. Which of the following best describes the legal position?

   A   An agency of necessity has arisen because Stephen is unable to contact Anthony

   B   An agency of necessity has arisen because there is an emergency situation and a pressing need for action

   C   No agency of necessity has arisen because the Rolls Royce is not a perishable good and Stephen's action was not reasonable

   D   No agency of necessity has arisen because there is no pre-existing contractual relationship between Stephen and Anthony   LO 1c

5   Preparing for her 40th birthday party, Scarlett went into Choice Wines and ordered three cases of pinot noir, saying that she was buying them in her capacity as agent for Dame Hilda, a well-known celebrity who lived in the same village and who was planning a summer ball in the grounds of her country house. Choice Wines supplied the wine and then invoiced Dame Hilda.

   Is there an agency by holding out or estoppel?

   A   Yes

   B   No

   Can Choice Wines demand payment from Dame Hilda?

   C   Yes

   D   No   LO 1c

6   Abigail is Peter's agent, authorised to buy local produce for sale in his farm shop. Despite the fact that Peter always told Abigail not to buy cheese, she meets with a local cheesemaker and orders, on Peter's behalf, 20 kilograms of smoked cheese, which she thinks is delicious and because she is convinced that it will be popular with customers. She also orders 7 kilograms of walnut and pickle brie. Peter likes the smoked cheese but finds the brie disgusting.

   Can he choose to ratify the contract in so far as it relates to the smoked cheese only?

   A   Yes

   B   No

   Will the effect of any ratification by the principal mean that the agent has no liability on the contract?

   C   Yes

   D   No   LO 1c

7   Andrea purchases ten watercolour paintings from an artist, Ross, for her employer, the Earl of Somerset, even though he has told her not to buy any more watercolours on his behalf but to concentrate on pastels. When the artist learns this, he demands their return as he had no wish for his work to hang in Andrea's terraced home in Bridgwater. However, the Earl of Somerset had come to like them after seeing them on Andrea's walls and refused the artist's demand for their return, sending him a cheque instead.

Does the Earl of Somerset's action amount to ratification of the contract?

A   Yes

B   No

Is the artist able to insist on the return of the watercolour paintings?

C   Yes

D   No   LO 1c

8   Are the following statements true or false?

On ratification of an agent's contract by a principal, the third party may then choose whether to enforce the contract against the agent or the principal.

A   True

B   False

Ratification can only validate an agent's past acts and will not endow any future authority.

C   True

D   False   LO 1c

9   Frank acts as an agent for Marilyn, purchasing silk nightwear from a number of different suppliers. Sometimes the suppliers pay a commission on orders placed with them by Frank on behalf of Marilyn. Frank regards the commissions as a perk of the job and keeps them. Which of the following best describes the legal position?

A   The commissions are regarded as bribes and Marilyn should report Frank to the police

B   Marilyn may dismiss Frank and recover the amount of commissions retained by him

C   Commissions are customarily retained by an agent as part of his remuneration and so Frank has no liability in respect of them

D   Marilyn can take action against the suppliers for directing the commissions to Frank instead of her   Sample Paper LO 1d

10   With regard to the duties owed by an agent:

Is an agent entitled to delegate the tasks that they are appointed to undertake, as they see fit?

A   Yes

B   No

Is an agent at liberty to reveal details about their principal discovered during the course of the agency relationship, once that relationship has ended?

C   Yes

D   No   LO 1d

11   Are the following statements true or false?

An agent is under a duty not to put themselves in a position where their interests conflict with those of their principal.

A   True

B   False

An agent must meet a standard of care and skill to be expected of a person in their profession.

C   True

D   False   LO 1d

12   Brian has just terminated his appointment of Livvi, who has been his agent for the past six months. The written contract of agency did not mention anything about remuneration and Brian relies on this when he refuses to pay her in respect of her services. He does, however, accept that he must reimburse her for £5,000 expenses that she has paid along the way.

Can Brian rely on the written contract to claim that no remuneration is payable to Livvi?

A   Yes

B   No

Is Livvi entitled to retain the goods belonging to Brian that she has in her possession until he pays her the sums owed to her?

C   Yes

D   No   Sample Paper LO 1d

13   Barnaby is a partner in Brown & Co, a dentists' practice. He orders four filing cabinets, one for reception and one for each of the surgeries, from Office Gear. The other two dentists in the practice think that this is an unnecessary expense and ask Office Gear to cancel the order. Office Gear is not prepared to do so and demands payment. Which of the following best describes the legal position as to whether or not Brown & Co is bound by the contract?

A   It is bound because the contract is within the implied usual authority of the dentist, Barnaby

B   It is bound because Office Gear knew that Barnaby was buying the cabinets for Brown & Co

C   It is not bound because Barnaby had authority to buy dentistry tools and equipment but not office supplies

D   It is not bound because the majority of partners do not wish to buy the cabinets   LO 1e

14 Amanda, Sophia and Nadia are in partnership, in the name of InStyle, providing interior design services to commercial clients. Sophia is a keen gardener and has advertised garden design and landscaping services, also in the name of InStyle. She has even carried out some gardening work and always puts up an InStyle sign at the entrance to the premises where she is working and Amanda and Nadia have not objected to Sophia putting up the sign and have not tried to stop her. In fact, they have welcomed the extra income for the partnership. When Sophia damages a valuable statuette while carrying out some landscaping works, the owner threatens to sue the partnership. Which of the following best describes the legal position?

A   InStyle is not liable because Sophia's implied usual authority relates to the interior design work only

B   InStyle is not liable because Sophia is wrongly using the partnership name for what is effectively her own business

C   InStyle is liable because Sophia has ostensible authority to carry out gardening services on behalf of InStyle

D   InStyle is not liable because ostensible authority cannot arise without active representation on the principal's part; inactivity is not enough   Sample Paper LO 1d

15 Barry, Kelvin and Oscar were the directors of Suresend Ltd. No managing director had been appointed but Kelvin and Oscar were well aware that Barry behaved as if he were Suresend Ltd's managing director. In particular Kelvin and Oscar knew that Barry entered into contracts on behalf of the company, including regularly hiring cars and requiring valeting services from Fastfleet Ltd. Kevin and Oscar have now discovered that Barry has just entered into a contract with Fastfleet Ltd to service all Suresend's delivery vans and lorries. Kelvin and Barry do not wish Suresend Ltd to proceed with this contract with Fastfleet Ltd and claim that Barry had no authority to enter into the contract and have written to Fastfleet Ltd to this effect.

Which of the following best describes the legal position?

A   Suresend is not bound because it provided written revocation of the authority given to Barry

B   Suresend is not bound because Barry did not have actual authority

C   Suresend is bound because Barry had ostensible authority

D   Suresend is bound because Fastfleet relied on Barry's representations   LO 1e

16 Are the following statements true or false in connection with agency by estoppel?

The third party must show that they have relied on a representation that the contracting party was acting as agent for their principal.

A   True

B   False

It is not necessary to show that the claimant's loss was caused by their reliance on the representation.

C   True

D   False   LO 1c

17 Are the following statements true or false?

For an agency by estoppel to arise, there must be a pre-existing agency relationship between the principal and the agent.

A   True

B   False

When an individual revokes the authority of their agent they should inform the third parties, who regularly deal with the agent, of the change in circumstances in order to prevent the former agent having any continuing authority to act on their behalf.

C   True

D   False   LO 1c, 1e

18 Roz works in the accounts department of Bizzy Lizzy, a successful florist's business. The principal owner of the business, Vincent, was due to visit a specialist rose grower on the Isles of Scilly but was unable to go due to illness. Vincent asked Roz to go along instead. He telephoned the rose grower to say that his buying partner would be taking his place. Roz ordered 500 roses for Bizzy Lizzy. Which of the following best describes the legal position?

A   Roz had ostensible authority to order the roses

B   Roz had implied authority to order the roses

C   Roz had express authority to order the roses

D   Roz had no authority to order the roses   LO 1e

19 Annabel is Phil's agent. She enters into a contract with Tim, within her authority, expressly describing herself as an agent for Phil.

Can Annabel be liable on this contract with Tim?

A   Yes

B   No

If Annabel enters into a contract, saying that she is acting as agent but without actually naming Phil as her principal, does that mean that Phil will not be liable on the contract?

C   Yes

D   No   LO 1e

20 Ashley is Phyllis's agent and enters into a contract for the purchase of a vintage car from Vince, as instructed by Phyllis. Vince does not know that Ashley is buying the car for Phyllis, at the time of entering into the contract, but discovers this to be the case one week later.

If Vince then defaults on the sale, can Phyllis take action on the contract?

A   Yes

B   No

If Phyllis defaults on the purchase, can Vince take action on the contract?

C   Yes

D   No   LO 1e

21 Walter enters into a contract for the purchase of a barge from Barney. He is actually buying it for Natalie, although Barney does not know that Walter is buying it for anybody else (not that it would have made any difference to him). When the date for payment arrives, Walter is unable to pay for the barge and tells Barney that he was actually buying it for Natalie anyway. Is the contract enforceable against Natalie?

A   Yes

B   No

Is the contract enforceable against Walter?

C   Yes

D   No   LO 1e

22 Martha tells John that she wants to buy one of his horse sculptures on behalf of her grandmother, Lady Reynolds. In fact, Lady Reynolds has not asked her to do so. Three months later, John contacts Lady Reynolds to say that he has completed a bronze stallion and it is ready for collection on the payment of £10,000. Lady Reynolds denies all knowledge of it and refuses to pay.

Can John sue Lady Reynolds on the contract?

A   Yes

B   No

Can John sue Martha under the tort of deceit?

C   Yes

D   No   LO 1c, 1e

23 A valid agency relationship can be created by:

Express appointment

A   Yes

B   No

Ratification

C   Yes

D   No   LO 1c

24 Dennis was a partner in Doolittle Solicitors. He retires from the partnership and the firm's existing clients and suppliers are informed of this fact; the firm amends its stationery so that Dennis's name no longer appears on it. A short time later, Dennis orders goods using old stationery which still has his name on it and asks for the bill to be sent to Doolittle Solicitors.

Which of the following statements is correct?

A   There is a binding contract between Dennis and the firm which supplied the goods

B   No binding contract has been created between the supplier and Doolittle Solicitors because Dennis was not authorised to act on behalf of the firm

C   There is a binding contract between Doolittle Solicitors and the firm which supplied the goods

D   No binding contract has been created because the partnership shown on the stationery had ceased to exist   Sample Paper LO 1c

25 An agent's authority to act on behalf of their principal can arise:

Where express authority is explicitly granted by the principal to the agent.

A   Yes

B   No

Where a person with actual authority makes a representation to a third party that a particular person has the authority to act as their agent without actually appointing the agent.

C   Yes

D   No

Sample Paper LO 1e

Chapter 4: Negligence

1   Are the following statements true or false?

The measure of damages in a contract is such an amount as would restore the party to the position they were in before the breach of contract.

A   True

B   False

The measure of damages in tort is such an amount as would put the party in the position they would have been in, if the tort had not been committed.

C   True

D   False   LO 1f

2   In respect of a successful action in the tort of negligence:

Is it true that the claimant must have suffered personal injury?

A   Yes

B   No

Is the standard of proof the balance of probabilities?

C   Yes

D   No   LO 1f

3   In an action for negligence:

Does there need to be some sort of pre-existing relationship between the claimant and defendant at the time of the act complained of, although not necessarily a contractual relationship?

A   Yes

B   No

Does the court need to be satisfied that public policy would allow a duty of care to exist?

C   Yes

D   No   LO 1f

4   Which of the following is irrelevant in determining whether a duty of care exists?

A   Whether it is fair that the law should impose a duty on the defendant

B   Whether the defendant intended to cause injury to the claimant

C   Whether it was reasonably foreseeable that the claimant might suffer damage as a result of the defendant's actions

D   Whether there is sufficient proximity between the parties   LO 1f

5   Which of the following statements is incorrect?

   A   If the defendant succeeds in arguing *res ipsa loquitur*, the burden of proof is then on the claimant to show negligence

   B   In arguing *res ipsa loquitur*, it must be shown that the thing that caused the damage was under the management and control of the defendant

   C   *Res ipsa loquitur* is relevant where the reason for the damage is not known

   D   Whether a breach of the duty of care has occurred is a matter of fact   LO 1f

6   Anton is learning to drive with his father, when he mistakenly goes into reverse gear instead of first gear, and hits a pedestrian on the road behind him. Although he is moving very slowly, the elderly and frail pedestrian suffers bruising, but also a heart attack induced by the shock. She dies within minutes. Which of the following best describes the legal position?

   A   The standard of care owed by Anton is that of a reasonable learner driver and the fact that she is especially vulnerable is irrelevant

   B   The standard of care owed is that of a reasonable driver and it is irrelevant that she was especially vulnerable

   C   The standard of care owed is that of a reasonable learner driver but the fact that she was especially vulnerable means that a higher standard will be applied

   D   The standard of care owed is that of a reasonable driver but the fact that she was especially vulnerable means that a higher standard will be applied   LO 1f

7   Natasha holds all relevant qualifications in horse and stable management. She runs a stable yard and has a team of college students to help at the yard, including transferring horses from the stables to the field and vice versa. One day, Becky, a student, went to collect a horse and was kicked in the head. She suffered serious injury. Shortly after this incident, a similar incident happened at the yard of a top showjumper. Reacting to this later incident, the Horse Society issued a direction that all yard owners should ensure that their grooms and helpers always wear suitable headgear when turning out or catching horses. After reading this, Becky's parents decide to sue Natasha for negligence. In the context of negligence:

   Is the Horse Society guidance relevant to the standard of care owed by Natasha?

   A   Yes

   B   No

   Is the standard of care owed by Natasha that of an ordinary reasonable man guided by those considerations that normally regulate the conduct of human affairs?

   C   Yes

   D   No   LO 1f

8   Winston is a fireman. On a recent call out to a major fire, he sped through red traffic lights and injured a cyclist as a result. Winston provides you with a copy of an article in a publication of a Firefighters' Organisation, written by a fellow fireman, saying that going through a red light is acceptable practice on the way to an incident, but not on the way back. Are the following statements true or false?

The fact that Winston was responding to an emergency will be taken into account in assessing the standard of care owed by him.

A   True

B   False

The article is evidence of professional opinion that supports his action and will negate any potential liability that he may have.

C   True

D   False   LO 1f

9   John drives in a careless fashion down a narrow street with cars parked on each side of the road, actually knocking the wing mirrors off two of the cars. While Naomi is watching him, she trips on some tools that have been left out by council workmen laying new kerbstones and breaks her ankle. Which of the following best describes the legal position?

A   John is liable because his negligent driving causes her to trip

B   Naomi is liable because she does not look where she is going

C   The local authority is liable because its workers are negligent in leaving tools on the pavement

D   John and the local authority are both liable because they both caused her injury   LO 1f

10 An accountant has given incorrect tax advice to one of their clients. The error on the part of the accountant constituted negligence. Do they face potential liability in:

A   contract only?

B   tort only?

C   contract and tort?

D   neither contract nor tort, but in misrepresentation?   LO 1f

11 Brown & Cameron, a firm of accountants, prepares accounts for Target plc, showing a profit of £800,000 when they should, in fact, have shown a loss of £8,000. Marnie owned 300 shares in the company and, after reading the accounts that were sent to her (as to all shareholders), she purchased an additional 500 shares. When it came to light that the accounts had been prepared negligently (and the share price tumbled as a result of that negligence), Marnie sued the accountants for negligence. There was no disclaimer of liability in the audit report. Which of the following best describes the legal position in respect of the potential liability of the firm, Brown & Cameron to Marnie?

A It is liable because the partners in the firm knew that the accounts would be sent to all shareholders

B It is liable because it was reasonably foreseeable that existing shareholders would rely on the accounts for the purpose of reviewing their investments

C It is not liable because Marnie bought her shares on the Stock Exchange and not from the company

D It is not liable because the firm did not owe a duty to existing shareholders who rely on the accounts for a purpose other than that for which they were intended   LO 1f

12 Campbells, a firm of accountants, prepared annual accounts for Thespians plc. The director of Moneymakers Ltd, which held shares in Thespians plc, saw the accounts and, as a result, the company lent Thespians plc £100,000 to finance its new premises. In fact, the accounts had been prepared negligently and Thespians plc was actually facing mounting debts. Since there was no disclaimer of liability in the audit report, Moneymakers Ltd sued Campbells. Which of the following best describes the legal position regarding Campbells' potential liability to Moneymakers Ltd?

A Campbells is liable because it owes a duty of care to potential lenders

B Campbells is liable because it knew that Moneymakers Ltd was a shareholder and would therefore have sight of the accounts

C Campbells is not liable because the accounts were not prepared for the purpose of enabling people to decide whether or not to lend to the company

D Campbells is not liable because such a lender should have investigated the accounts and concluded that they were inaccurate   LO 1f

13 Malcolm is managing director of Eastreach Ltd. Knowing that the finance director, Finley, was undergoing cancer treatment, Malcolm asked Tristan, an accountant, to prepare the company's accounts. Tristan provided the accounts in draft and Malcolm asked Finley to check that he was happy with them. While awaiting Finley's review, George, Tristan's brother (and business rival), saw the draft accounts and bought the entire 51% shareholding in Eastreach Ltd owned by Brigitte. When Finley had finished checking the accounts, it was discovered that Tristan had made significant accounting errors and had shown the company to be significantly more profitable than it was: in fact the company was heading for insolvency. Brigitte is delighted but George sues Tristan for his negligence, noting that Tristan had not made any disclaimer of liability in respect of his work. Which of the following statements is incorrect?

A Tristan owed a duty of care because George was known to him

B Tristan owed no duty of care because he did not know that George would look at the accounts

C Tristan owed a duty of care to Malcolm

D Tristan owed no duty of care to Brigitte   LO 1f

14 Tina, a trainee accountant, was approached by Kevin, the husband of Tina's senior colleague, Jill, at an office party. Kevin asked her for some professional advice. Flattered that he had asked her rather than Jill, Tina obliged. However, her advice was flawed. Is she liable for the resulting loss suffered by Kevin?

A No, because she is only a trainee

B No, because the advice was not given in a professional context

C Yes, because she knows him and assumes responsibility for her advice

D Yes, because she owes a duty of care for which the standard is that of a reasonable qualified accountant

LO 1f

15 Tim, an accountant, prepares financial statements for MarkUp plc, knowing that the company was considering three takeover bids, including one from Growth plc. There was no disclaimer of liability in the accounts. In the event that Tim prepares the statements negligently, indicating that the company is financially secure when it is not, and Growth plc takes over MarkUp plc on the basis of those accounts:

Can Growth plc recover any resulting losses it makes on the takeover?

A Yes

B No

Will Tim be liable to pay damages to the other takeover bidders where they were also identified to him as potential takeover bidders who would be relying on the accounts?

C Yes

D No

LO 1f

16 Are the following statements true or false?

An auditor who is responsible for an auditor's report containing materially false or misleading information commits an offence under the Companies Act 2006 that is punishable by a fine and/or imprisonment.

A True

B False

A liability limitation agreement between a company and its auditor limiting potential liability for negligence in the course of auditing accounts is automatically void.

C True

D False

LO 1f

17 With regard to an auditor's potential liability in tort for providing audited accounts:

Is a provision (other than in a liability limitation agreement) that excludes them from such liability enforceable?

A Yes

B No

Can the company agree to indemnify an auditor against such liability?

C Yes

D No

LO 1f

18 Esther sues Nathan for negligence. The court finds that Nathan was guilty of negligence but that Esther was equally to blame. Esther has suffered a loss of £30,000. Which of the following is accurate?

    A   Nathan must pay damages of £30,000 to Esther because, although blameworthy, she would not have suffered any loss but for his negligence

    B   Nathan must pay damages of £15,000

    C   Nathan is not liable to pay damages because Esther's loss would not have been so great but for her own negligence

    D   The courts will consider all the circumstances of the case to determine the proportion of the loss that Nathan should pay
    LO 1f

19 Neil is a private pilot. After celebrating receiving his private pilot's licence, he drinks two bottles of champagne. He then offers a lift to his teetotal girlfriend, Kate, back to her family residence in the country where her father has a small airfield. Kate accepts, even though she knows that he has drunk two bottles of champagne. Neil crashes the plane and Kate breaks her neck. Which of the following best describes the legal position?

    A   Neil has no liability because *volenti non fit injuria* applies

    B   *Volenti* does not apply but Neil's liability may be reduced on the grounds of contributory negligence

    C   Neil is not liable because Kate knew well the risk that she was taking

    D   Neil is not liable because Kate consented to taking a risk
    LO 1f

20 The Unfair Contract Terms Act 1977 provides that a person who is acting in the course of a business cannot exclude liability for any consequences of any negligent act on their part.

    A   True

    B   False

The Unfair Contract Terms Act 1977 does not apply to a clause excluding liability for negligence which has agreed between two businesses.

    C   True

    D   False
    LO 1f

21 With regard to damages for negligence, do the following matters have to be considered to be reasonably foreseeable, in order that the claimant can recover damages in respect of their loss?

The manner in which the loss was suffered.

    A   Yes

    B   No

The extent of the loss.

    C   Yes

    D   No
    LO 1f

22 Are the following statements true or false?

A principal is liable for the acts of his agent, provided they are committed by the agent in the course of performing the task for which they are an agent.

A   True

B   False

An employer will not be vicariously liable for the negligent acts of their employee, provided they can show that they took reasonable steps to avert the possibility of the tort being committed.

C   True

D   False   LO 1g

23 Nigel is an accountant working for Portillo & Co. While visiting a client's business premises for the purposes of an audit, he recognised one of the client's office staff, Wayne, as the person responsible for his latest love affair ending. When Wayne walked past, Nigel went to punch him but Wayne ducked and Nigel hit Alice instead, breaking her nose.

Is Nigel liable in tort?

A   Yes

B   No

Is Portillo & Co vicariously liable?

C   Yes

D   No   LO 1g

24 Reg is a bus driver and is bound by his employer's rules that say he must not race other bus drivers. However, he does so and causes personal injury to Tabatha who is crossing the road.

Is Reg acting in the course of his employment?

A   Yes

B   No

Is Reg's employer vicariously liable for his act?

C   Yes

D   No   LO 1g

25 Alice is a newly qualified accountant employed in an accountancy firm. An old friend, Bashir, meets her at a party and asks for some tax advice. Alice tells him to make an appointment to see her in the office which he does. Alice advises him on his tax affairs. This advice misinterprets certain statutory provisions relating to tax. Bashir relies on the advice and loses money. A reasonably competent accountant would not have given the advice which Alice gave.

If Alice is sued for negligence, could she could rely on any of the following factors as a complete or partial defence:

She was newly qualified and could not be expected to reach the same standard of competence as a more experienced accountant.

A Yes

B No

Bashir would have suffered the loss even if the advice had been correct.

C Yes

D No   Sample Paper LO 1f

26 Susan is a newly qualified accountant employed in an accountancy firm, Calculator LLP. Susan advised Tariq on his tax affairs and Tariq lost a substantial sum of money. Tariq wants to bring a claim for this loss. Which of the following is correct?

A He could sue Susan if her advice was incorrect

B He could sue Calculator LLP if Susan's advice was incorrect

C He could sue Susan or Calculator LLP if Susan's advice was negligent

D He could sue neither Susan nor Calculator LLP since his loss was purely financial

Sample Paper LO 1g

27 Rustom owned shares in Target plc. In January 20X0 he bought a further 10,000 shares in Target plc after reading the following:

(1) A newspaper column by Tipster which stated that Target plc was a company which would benefit from the predicted rise in house prices in 20X0

(2) A post card sent by a friend, Carl, who stated that he had paid for his holiday with his dividends from Target plc

(3) The annual accounts of Target plc which had been signed off by Target's auditors, Laylem LLP

Within a month of Rustom buying the extra shares Target plc went into insolvent liquidation and he wants to know if any of Tipster, Carl or Laylem LLP owe him a duty of care in respect of his purchase of the 10,000 shares.

A Tipster, Carl and Laylem LLP all owe Rustom a duty of care

B None of Tipster, Carl or Laylem LLP owe Rustom a duty of care

C Only Laylem LLP owe Rustom a duty of care

D Both Carl and Tipster owe Rustom a duty of care   Sample Paper LO 1f

28 When an employee commits a tort his employer may be found to be vicariously liable. Which of the following best describes vicarious liability?

   A   Vicarious liability arises when the employee's tort is committed in the course of his employment. The principal purpose of the imposition of vicarious liability on an employer is to punish the employer for employing a negligent employee

   B   Vicarious liability arises when the employee's tort is committed in the course of his employment. The principal purpose of the imposition of vicarious liability on an employer is to ensure the victim of the tort has a solvent person against whom the victim can bring a claim

   C   Vicarious liability arises when the employee commits a tort irrespective of whether it is committed in the course of his employment. The principal purpose of the imposition of vicarious liability on an employer is to punish the employer for employing a negligent employee

   D   Vicarious liability arises when the employee commits a tort irrespective of whether it is committed in the course of his employment. The principal purpose of the imposition of vicarious liability on an employer is to ensure the victim of the tort has a solvent person against whom the victim can bring a claim   Sample Paper LO 1g

29 Zebra & Co is a firm of accountants whose audit clients include Widget plc. During the course of Widget plc's last audit Zebra & Co sent a new recruit, Oliver, to check Widget plc's stock control systems; Oliver failed to notice some irregularities in the procedures adopted by Widget plc.

   Relying on the published accounts which Zebra & Co had approved, Priya, bought shares in Widget plc. Within a month the shares had dropped in value by £4,000 and Priya wants to sue Zebra & Co to recover her loss.

   Which of the following best represents Priya's position?

   A   She can sue Zebra & Co because the firm owes her a duty of care and Oliver failed to notice the flaws in the stock control system

   B   Even though Zebra & Co owes her a duty of care she cannot sue Zebra & Co unless she can prove that Oliver's failure to spot the flaws caused her loss

   C   She can sue Zebra & Co because the firm owes her a duty of care and Oliver must be judged by the standard of a more experienced accountant

   D   She cannot sue Zebra & Co because the firm does not owe a duty of care to potential purchasers of shares in Widget plc   Sample Paper LO 1f

30 Where it can be shown that A owes B a contractual duty of care, it follows that a duty of care is also owed in tort.

   A   True

   B   False

   In a claim for negligent misstatement, it will be harder for a sophisticated investor to satisfy the court that an auditor owes them a duty of care.

   C   True

   D   False   LO 1f

Chapter 5: Companies: the consequences of incorporation

1   With regard to limited liability, answer the following:

Is one of the main advantages of a registered company, the fact that it may enjoy limited liability?

A   Yes

B   No

In the event of a registered company limited by shares being wound up, are its members always required to pay the outstanding amount of any share premium payable in respect of their shares, in addition to any outstanding part of their nominal value?

C   Yes

D   No   LO 2a

2   Mark incorporates his sole trader business, King Kilts, which manufactures high quality tartan kilts and sporrans, under the name King Kilts Ltd. He lent King Kilts Ltd £20,000 and owns 95% of its shares. He continued to insure the company's assets, including the factory, in his own name, as he had always done before incorporation. On New Year's Eve, the factory was destroyed by fire. Which of the following best describes the legal position?

A   Mark can claim on the insurance because King Kilts Ltd is essentially no different from the original business

B   Mark can claim on the insurance because he has an insurable interest as a creditor of King Kilts Ltd

C   Mark can claim on the insurance because he has an insurable interest as a member of King Kilts Ltd

D   Mark cannot claim on the insurance because the insurance is not effected in the name of King Kilts Ltd and the company has the insurable interest   Sample Paper LO 2a

3   In some cases, the court lifts the corporate veil, for example to ignore the incorporated nature of a business altogether in those cases where it appears to be nothing but a sham. Are the courts likely to lift the corporate veil in the following situations?

Where the creditors of a subsidiary company are unlikely to receive settlement of their debts even though the holding company is financially very secure?

A   Yes

B   No

Where a company is registered in England and Wales but all its members, except one, belong to Neverland, a country with which England is at war? The company has five members with equal shareholdings.

C   Yes

D   No   LO 2a

4   Are the following statements true or false?

Where a public limited company fails to obtain a trading certificate, a member-director may be personally liable as a result. This is one example of statute lifting the corporate veil.

A   True

B   False

A company is always liable without limit for its own debts.

C   True

D   False   LO 2a

5   Leo and Seamus are planning to set up a public company selling electrical goods at discounted rates. They ask for your advice on the following matters:

Can it be an unlimited company?

A   Yes

B   No

Can the company commence trading once it is incorporated, provided they obtain a trading certificate within the first 12 months following incorporation?

C   Yes

D   No   LO 2a, 2b

6   Ashley and George, the directors of Pending Ltd, a fantastically successful company with a high public profile, plan to re-register their company as a public limited company. They have never had a company secretary before because Ashley has always dealt with that side of things. The company has a share capital of £50,000.

Do they need to appoint a company secretary?

A   Yes

B   No

Do they need to increase the share capital of the company?

C   Yes

D   No   LO 2a, 2b

7   Which of the following statements is incorrect?

A   A private company cannot offer its securities to the public

B   Only a private limited company can pass written resolutions

C   Public and private limited companies must have at least two directors

D   A private limited company does not need to hold an annual general meeting   LO 2a

8   Within what time period following the end of the relevant accounting reference period must a public limited company file its accounts and reports?

    A   Five months

    B   Six months

    C   Seven months

    D   Nine months   LO 2c

---

9   Which of the following statements is correct only in respect of a public limited company?

    A   The company may exclude rights of pre-emption

    B   The company may reduce its share capital subject to obtaining a special resolution and providing a directors' declaration of solvency

    C   Shares must be at least one quarter paid up on allotment

    D   The company may redeem its shares out of its own share capital, subject to its articles of association   LO 2a, 2c

---

10   Are the following statements true or false?

When a company applies for registration, a copy of its proposed articles of association must be supplied to the Registrar of Companies.

    A   True

    B   False

A certificate of incorporation is conclusive evidence that a company is registered in accordance with the Companies Act 2006.

    C   True

    D   False   LO 2b

---

11   Paddy arranges for the registration of New Style Ltd. Before the company is incorporated, he enters into a contract on its behalf for the purchase of premises at a prime retail location. When the time comes for completion of the purchase, the vendor refuses to complete the transaction with New Style Ltd (which is now incorporated) as a matter of principle, because it dislikes some of the merchandise that New Style Ltd proposes to sell.

Can New Style Ltd enforce the contract against the vendor?

    A   Yes

    B   No

Can New Style Ltd ratify the contract for the purchase of the premises?

    C   Yes

    D   No   LO 2b, 2c

---

12 Quentin sets up a new company, Simple Solutions Ltd, to continue his existing business. Before Simple Solutions Ltd is incorporated, he enters into a contract on its behalf for the purchase of stock with payment to be made 30 days later. When the payment date arrives, the newly registered company has no cash available because it has also committed large funds to taking a lease of its new premises.

Can the seller of the stock enforce the contract against Simple Solutions Ltd?

A   Yes

B   No

Can the seller enforce the contract against Quentin?

C   Yes

D   No   LO 2b, 2c

13 With regard to a company changing its name, answer the following:

Can a company choose to change its name by special resolution for any reason at any time?

A   Yes

B   No

Can a registered company be ordered to change its name by the Registrar of Companies?

C   Yes

D   No   LO 2c

14 Josephine was one of two directors (who were also members) of Tone-Up Ltd, a supplier of health and fitness products. She did the administrative work in relation to setting up the company. She included a provision in its articles that Tone-Up Ltd would always employ her as its company secretary on a salary of £12,000 p.a. She also had a separate contract appointing her as company secretary, but it made no mention of remuneration or termination. After a year, Tone-Up Ltd appointed John as company secretary and Josephine sued the company for breach of contract because the articles had been contravened and, she argued, the articles have contractual effect.

Can Josephine rely on the articles to compel Tone-Up Ltd to pay her £12,000 p.a. in the absence of a term in her contract, during her period of office as company secretary?

A   Yes

B   No

Can Josephine rely on the contractual effect of the articles to seek redress for breach of contract?

C   Yes

D   No   LO 2b

15 Are the following statements true or false?

A company's articles of association can be altered by the passing of an ordinary resolution unless there is a provision for entrenchment, in which case a special resolution is required.

A   True

B   False

A company may provide that a provision for entrenchment cannot be repealed.

C   True

D   False   LO 2b

16 Simon is a solicitor employed by Xcel Ltd. He also owns 5% of the shares in the company. His contract is silent as to remuneration but Xcel Ltd's articles provide that the company's solicitor will receive £10,000 p.a. In August, the company passes a resolution altering the articles to reduce the solicitor's remuneration to £8,000 p.a. and to require all members to purchase 50 more shares at £5 each.

Is the alteration of the articles to reduce the solicitor's remuneration effective?

A   Yes

B   No

Is Simon, in his capacity as company member, required to take up the extra 50 shares?

C   Yes

D   No   LO 2b

17 With regard to the statutory books and records of a registered company limited by shares, answer the following:

Is a company required to keep a register of its directors' residential addresses?

A   Yes

B   No

Is a company required to keep a register of debenture-holders?

C   Yes

D   No   LO 2c

18 Mark is the company secretary of Top Tents Ltd, a private company limited by shares. He seeks your advice on the following matters:

Must the company provide a directors' remuneration report?

A   Yes

B   No

Must he file accounts and reports within nine months after the end of the relevant accounting reference period?

C   Yes

D   No   LO 2c

19 Tiny Tots Ltd employs 20 people and has a turnover of £11 million and a balance sheet showing £5.5 million.

Does the company qualify as a small company?

A   Yes

B   No

Must it appoint an auditor to carry out an audit of its annual accounts?

C   Yes

D   No   LO 2e

20 Craig is the company secretary of Lotsaland Ltd. He regularly negotiates contracts for the company for the acquisition of small development plots and then passes the file on to the managing director, Malcolm, who enters into the contract on behalf of the company. Feeling under pressure to secure a particularly good deal on a site during Malcolm's sabbatical, Craig enters into a contract for Lotsaland Ltd to borrow £15,000 so that it can secure the deal. When Malcolm returns, he is not happy with the borrowing arrangement made by Craig. Which of the following best describes the legal position?

A   Lotsaland Ltd is bound because Craig has ostensible authority to enter into the contract

B   Lotsaland Ltd is bound because Craig has the implied actual authority of a company secretary

C   Lotsaland Ltd is not bound by the borrowing contract, because the lender should have checked whether Craig had sufficient authority

D   Lotsaland Ltd is not bound because Craig lacked sufficient authority   LO 2c

21 Albert entered into a pre-incorporation contract on behalf of Stir Ltd. By whom and against whom may the contract be enforced?

A   By and against the company only

B   By and against Albert only

C   By the company and against Albert

D   Against the company and by Albert   Sample Paper LO 2b, 2c

22 Under the Companies Act 2006 essential requirements for registration as a private company limited by shares by the Registrar of Companies include the submission of:

The memorandum of association

A   Yes

B   No

A section 761 Trading Certificate

C   Yes

D   No   LO 2b

23 A properly appointed company secretary usually has the authority to:

Sign contracts connected with the administrative side of a company's affairs, such as employing staff and ordering cars

A   True

B   False

Sign contracts connected with the purchase of property on behalf of a company

C   True

D   False   Sample Paper LO 2c

24 Cabbit Ltd buys organic vegetables from growers and resells them to retail outlets. The Companies Act 2006 requires every company to keep adequate accounting records. In order to comply with this requirement of the Act, Cabbit Ltd's accounting records must contain:

(1)   a record of its assets and liabilities

(2)   a statement of stock held by the company at the end of each financial year

(3)   daily entries of income and expenditure

A   All of the above

B   None of the above

C   (1) and (2) only

D   (1) and (3) only   Sample Paper LO 2c

25 Whimsome Ltd has a turnover of £10 million, a balance sheet total of £5 million and employs 100 people. Within how many months of its year-end must the company file its annual accounts with the Registrar?

A   3 months

B   6 months

C   9 months

D   12 months   LO 2e

26 Micro-entities do not have to file a profit and loss account with the registrar.

A   True

B   False

Micro-entities do not have to file notes to the accounts with the registrar.

C   True

D   False   LO 2e

27   Which of the following companies is not required to appoint an auditor?

   A   A small-sized insurance company

   B   A medium-sized company

   C   A quoted company

   D   A not-for-profit company that is subject to public sector audit   LO 2e

Chapter 6: Companies: ownership and management

1   Which of the following types of director is normally appointed by ordinary resolution passed by the company members?

     A   De facto director

     B   Shadow director

     C   Alternate director

     D   Non-executive director   LO 2k

2   With regard to company directors and directors' powers, are the following statements true or false?

     The duties owed by a de facto director are the same as those of a properly appointed director.

     A   True

     B   False

     If a director's appointment is subsequently found to have been defective, their actions are invalidated as a result.

     C   True

     D   False   LO 2k, 2l

3   Are the following statements true or false?

     A sole director may also be company secretary but cannot also hold the position of the company's auditor.

     A   True

     B   False

     Subject to specific exceptions, a director should be at least 18 years old.

     C   True

     D   False   LO 2k

4   Bertie and Craig each own 30% of the shares in Vintage Cars Ltd. Digby owns 20% and Noel, the finance director, owns 20%. Bertie and Craig have become increasingly frustrated by Noel's apparent lack of vision for the company and are annoyed by a number of silly mistakes that he has made recently. They wish to remove him from the board of directors. Digby is undecided.

     Can Bertie and Craig remove Noel from the board without Digby's support?

     A   Yes

     B   No

     If Noel is removed from office, will his removal effect a lawful termination of his service contract as finance director?

     C   Yes

     D   No   LO 2k

5   Simon and his fellow directors Mark and Tom each own 100 of the 300 shares in Simple Pies Ltd. Under the articles of association, where a resolution is proposed to remove a director, that director is entitled to three votes per share. Mark and Tom vote to remove Simon but when a poll is taken, Simon defeats the resolution by 300 votes to 200. Which of the following best describes the legal position?

   A   Simon has not been removed because the weighted voting rights have been validly given and validly exercised

   B   Simon has been removed because the article giving weighted voting rights contravenes the Companies Act 2006 which enables a director to be removed on the passing of an ordinary resolution with special notice

   C   Simon has not been validly removed because the articles would effectively mean that a director could never be removed

   D   Simon has been validly removed because voting should not have been conducted by a poll on a resolution to remove a director
                                                                                                    LO 2k

6   Are the following statements true or false?

   A company must state its objects in its constitution, because directors can only exercise their powers in pursuance of those objects.

   A   True

   B   False

   Directors are agents of the members of the company for the purposes of managing the company's business.

   C   True

   D   False
                                                                                                    LO 2m

7   Frank is a director of Bridalwear Ltd. He has never been appointed as managing director formally, but for the past 10 years he has conducted the day to day business of the company as if he had been. The other directors and shareholders, Flora and Gail, have never objected as they have considered him to be doing a marvellous job. One day, a little out of character, he decides that the company should branch into selling floral bouquets and buttonholes for weddings as a sideline. He contracts to buy oasis and baskets to the value of £3,000. Which of the following best describes the legal position?

   A   Frank has acted with express authority as Flora and Gail allow him to do anything

   B   Frank has acted within his implied incidental authority, as the contract is incidental to the company's bridal wear business

   C   Frank has acted within the ostensible authority of a managing director to enter into all commercial contracts in relation to the company's business

   D   Frank has acted within his implied usual authority as managing director
                                                                                                    LO 2m

8   Mork is the managing director of Parallels Ltd, a company that deals in weird and wonderful gadgets. His co-directors and shareholders, Patik and Asif agree that he should buy some kaleidoscopes up to a total value of £200. Mork finds a supplier of kaleidoscopes, Weird Ltd that is offering a particular model of kaleidoscope new to the market. Mork thinks that the product is just fabulous and orders £275 worth. When the invoice arrives, Patik and Asif refuse to pay it because Mork has exceeded his authority. Which of the following best summarises the legal position?

   A   Parallels Ltd is not bound because Mork has acted beyond his authority

   B   Weird Ltd cannot enforce the contract, although it acted in good faith. Mork's authority was limited and Weird should have asked for evidence of his authority

   C   Parallels Ltd is bound because Mork had implied authority to enter into the contract

   D   Weird Ltd can enforce the contract because it dealt with Parallels Ltd in good faith   LO 2m

9   Are the following statements true or false?

   The statutory duty of a director to disclose any interest that they have in a proposed transaction or arrangement with the company does not apply to shadow directors.

   A   True

   B   False

   A director may not exercise their powers except for the purpose for which they were conferred.

   C   True

   D   False   LO 2l

10   Richard and Don owned 55% of the issued shares in Fasttrack Ltd. They learned that its directors Shivani and James were in talks with Ultrasonic Ltd in respect of a takeover of Fasttrack by Ultrasonic Ltd. They made known their views to the directors which were that the takeover would be disastrous in the long term for Fasttrack Ltd's business. Shivani and James disagreed and so they allotted some shares to Ultrasonic Ltd in order to reduce Richard's and Don's shareholdings to less than 50% (and not for the purpose of raising capital). Which of the following best describes the legal position?

   A   The allotment is valid because it is done within the powers granted to directors

   B   The allotment is valid because directors have ultimate control of management decisions

   C   The allotment is invalid as it is a principle of company law that the wishes of the majority prevail and in this case Richard and Don were majority shareholders

   D   The allotment is invalid because the directors have exercised their powers for a collateral purpose of destroying an existing majority   LO 2m

11 Are the following statements true or false?

The duty to exercise independent judgement overrides any agreement or provision that restricts or fetters the exercise of discretion by a director.

A   True

B   False

A director may accept a benefit from a third party by reason of their being a director, provided the acceptance of the benefit cannot reasonably be regarded as likely to give rise to a conflict of interest.

C   True

D   False   LO 2I

12 The Companies Act 2006 provides that a director must avoid a situation in which he has a direct or indirect interest that conflicts with the interests of the company, unless it is authorised by the company's other directors. Assuming that the articles do not invalidate any purported authorisation by the directors:

Can directors authorise such a conflict in a private company?

A   Yes

B   No

Can directors authorise such a conflict in a public company (in the absence of any express provision in the articles)?

C   Yes

D   No   LO 2I

13 Farah is a director of In Tunes Ltd, a company selling modern sheet music and a small range of musical instruments. He is also a FCA with 20 years' experience as an accountant in private practice. Nathaniel is also a director. He ran his own retail business for ten years but doesn't play much part in the management of the business of In Tunes Ltd, except that he attends board meetings. He tends to leave the routine conduct of the business in the hands of Farah and Amy, the finance director.

Is Farah's personal skill and experience as a chartered accountant relevant to the standard of care that he must demonstrate as a company director?

A   Yes

B   No

Is Nathaniel acting in breach of his director's duty to exercise reasonable care, skill and diligence, since he has not concerned himself with the company's affairs in between board meetings?

C   Yes

D   No   LO 2I

14 The managing director of King Kitchens Ltd presents a proposal to the board of directors for the purchase of the complete stock of Integral Inspirations Ltd, which is being wound up. Neville, one of the directors, is also a director of Integral Inspirations Ltd. In view of the possible conflict of interest, he discloses his interest to the board. Assuming there is nothing in the company's articles of association:

Does Neville need to obtain the approval of the board?

A Yes

B No

Does Neville need to obtain the approval of members in general meeting?

C Yes

D No   LO 2I

---

15 Are the following statements true or false?

From the time when a director vacates office, they cease to be subject to any statutory duties as a company director.

A True

B False

Where a director enters into a contract with the company, in breach of their duties, the contract is rendered voidable at the option of the company.

C True

D False   LO 2I

---

16 Kim, Tamsin and Anna are directors of Teen Tunes Ltd. Kim and Tamsin have recently sold some of the company's assets to Top Trumps Ltd, a company in which they are the only directors and shareholders. They sold the assets, secretly, at less than their market value. Anna was not a party to the arrangements and is not in breach of any of the duties she owes as director. Which of the following best describes the legal position?

A Kim and Tamsin are jointly and severally liable to make good the loss suffered by Teen Tunes Ltd

B Kim, Tamsin and Anna are jointly liable to make good the loss suffered by Teen Tunes Ltd

C Kim, Tamsin and Anna are jointly and severally liable to make good the loss suffered by Teen Tunes Ltd

D Anna may avoid the contract between Teen Tunes Ltd and Top Trumps Ltd   LO 2I

---

17 Giles is the finance director of Super Sports Ltd and is responsible for insuring the business premises. When he receives an insurance proposal from the company's usual insurers, he signs and posts it by way of acceptance without ever reading it. Which of the following statements is incorrect?

A Giles will be liable for negligence

B The members of the company may ratify Giles' actions by ordinary resolution

C Giles' votes and those of any member connected with him must be disregarded for the purposes of any ratification

D Giles will not be liable if there is a provision excluding him from liability for negligence   LO 2I

18 Drake was formerly a director of two listed companies. He is now a director of Dark Side Ltd and actively manages his business in a way that prejudices the company's main creditor, Sunshine Bank plc, but favours a small number of smaller lenders with whom he has connections. The financial status of Dark Side Ltd is rapidly approaching a situation where it may be unable to pay its debts but it is not yet insolvent.

Can Drake be liable to contribute to the assets of the company by reason of his fraudulent trading?

A   Yes

B   No

Will the fact that he is a highly experienced businessman be relevant to the standard of care applied, if he were ever to be sued for wrongful trading?

C   Yes

D   No   LO 2l

19 Miles and Elizabeth are both directors of a private company selling organic food. Miles has been found guilty of a number of breaches of competition law. Elizabeth was also a director and company secretary of Big Beans Ltd, a company that has just gone into insolvent liquidation. The court is considering an application for their disqualification.

Will Miles face certain disqualification?

A   Yes

B   No

Will disqualification be automatic for Elizabeth?

C   Yes

D   No   LO 2k, 2l

20 Are the following statements true or false?

Any individual member can apply to the court for cancellation of a variation of class rights, provided they are a member of the class affected.

A   True

B   False

Holders of at least 10% of the company's paid up capital with voting rights can requisition a general meeting.

C   True

D   False   LO 2h

21 Andrew is a shareholder in Star Buys Ltd and is preparing to pursue a derivative claim in the court for breach of duty by Arthur and Edgar, two of the company's directors.

Must Andrew show that Arthur and Edgar control the majority of the company's shares?

A Yes

B No

Can Andrew pursue the claim where the relevant act or omission is authorised by the company beforehand or ratified by it subsequently?

C Yes

D No   LO 2i

22 Are the following statements true or false?

A company member may make an application for relief on the grounds of unfairly prejudicial conduct, even in respect of an act or omission that has not yet occurred, where they consider that the proposed act or omission will be unfairly prejudicial to the interests of the company's members.

A True

B False

Relief under s 994 will not be granted unless there has been a breach of company law.

C True

D False   LO 2i

23 Where someone is successful in applying for relief on the grounds of unfairly prejudicial conduct, which of the following orders might a court make?

(1) An order not to make any alteration of its articles of association without obtaining the permission of the court first

(2) An order regulating the future conduct of the company's affairs

(3) An order authorising legal proceedings to be brought on behalf of the company

A None

B All

C (1) and/or (2) only

D (2) and/or (3) only   LO 2i

24 Rupert is a member of Great Golf Ltd and is in dispute with the company. The majority agreed to buy out his interest in the company but no agreement as to the purchase price for his shares was ever reached. Exasperated by the actions of the majority, Rupert intends to petition the court on the grounds that it is just and equitable to wind up the company.

Is petitioning the court for winding up on the just and equitable ground available to any member regardless of the size of his shareholding?

A   Yes

B   No

Is the court likely to order the winding up of Great Golf Ltd on the just and equitable ground?

C   Yes

D   No   LO 2i

25 Shareholders representing what minimum percentage of the nominal value of shares with voting rights must agree to shorter notice than 14 days for a general meeting, in the absence of any provision in the articles of association?

A   51%

B   75%

C   90%

D   95%   LO 2h

26 How much notice is required to be given by a public limited company for the holding of its annual general meeting?

A   7 days

B   14 days

C   21 days

D   28 days   LO 2h

27 Are the following statements true or false?

A private company is not required to hold an annual general meeting.

A   True

B   False

A public limited company can use the written resolution procedure provided its articles of association expressly authorise it.

C   True

D   False   LO 2k, 2h

28 Which of the following actions requires the passing of an ordinary resolution with special notice?

    A   The change of company's name

    B   An alteration of a company's articles of association

    C   A reduction of a company's share capital

    D   The removal of an auditor   LO 2h

---

29 A director can be removed from office:

By passing a written resolution

    A   Yes

    B   No

Under a provision of a company's articles of association

    C   Yes

    D   No   Sample Paper LO 2k

---

30 The following conduct by a director constitutes a breach of duty:

Misusing confidential information relating to the company for their personal gain

    A   Yes

    B   No

Abusing a corporate opportunity

    C   Yes

    D   No   Sample Paper LO 2l

---

31 Lee is the managing director of ABC Carpets Ltd. Last month he signed a proposal for insurance against flood damage without reading it. The proposal had been filled in by his insurance broker and contained inaccurate answers to some questions. The insurers have now declined liability following a flood, which has destroyed most of the company's stock of carpets.

Is Lee in breach of his duty as a director?

    A   No, he has acted in good faith and exercised his powers as a company director constitutionally

    B   No, the insurance company are liable, it was their insurance broker who filled in the insurance form incorrectly

    C   Yes, in his capacity as managing director of ABC Carpets Ltd he should have checked that the insurance form was completed correctly before he signed it

    D   No, as long as he can show that he has exhibited the degree of skill which may reasonably be expected from a person of his knowledge and experience   Sample Paper LO 2l

32 Are the following statements true or false in relation to the exercise of director's powers?

A director of a company is required to exercise their powers subject to any directions given by ordinary resolution.

A   True

B   False

A director of a company can restrict the exercise of their power by agreeing in advance to support any resolution proposed by the majority shareholder.

C   True

D   False   Sample Paper LO 2m

33 Which of the following can be passed by ordinary resolution?

A   A change of company name

B   The alteration of the articles

C   The removal of a company director

D   A variation of class rights   Sample Paper LO 2h

34 Which, if any, of the following requirements must be met if an action for unfairly prejudicial conduct is to be successful?

(1) The company must be a public limited company

(2) There must be unfairly prejudicial conduct which affects all shareholders

(3) The conduct alleged to be unfairly prejudicial must relate to actions which are continuing at the time the action is brought

A   None of the above

B   All of the above

C   (1) and (2) only

D   (2) and (3) only   Sample Paper LO 2i

1 Which type of share carries the right to demand payment of a dividend?

   (1) Ordinary share

   (2) Preference share

   A   (1) only

   B   (2) only

   C   (1) and (2)

   D   Neither (1) nor (2)   LO 2d

2 Slither Ltd has both ordinary and preference shares. The articles of Slither Ltd do not specify what is to happen to surplus assets on winding up, after all creditors have been paid. Which shareholders, if any, are entitled to these surplus assets?

   (1) Ordinary shareholders

   (2) Preference shareholders

   A   (1) only

   B   (2) only

   C   (1) and (2)

   D   Neither (1) nor (2)   LO 2d

3 Are the following statements true or false?

Preference shares do not carry a right to vote unless express provision is made to that effect.

   A   True

   B   False

Ordinary shares carry statutory rights of pre-emption (unless lawfully excluded) but preference shares will only have pre-emption rights where such rights are conferred on them by the company's articles of association or terms of issue.

   C   True

   D   False   LO 2d

4   Atlas Ltd has ordinary and preference shares. The articles provide that the preference shares, carry a 10% preference dividend and that these shareholders have the right to appoint a consultant who is entitled to attend board meetings and speak on behalf of the preference shareholders. Only the preference shares carry these rights.

Is the right to receive a 10% dividend a 'class right'?

A   Yes

B   No

Is the right to appoint a 'consultant' a class right?

C   Yes

D   No   LO 2d

---

5   Following a variation of class rights, the holders of a certain percentage of the issued shares of the class in question may apply to the court to have the variation cancelled. What is that percentage?

A   20%

B   15%

C   10%

D   5%   LO 2d

---

6   Widgets Ltd had two classes of ordinary shares, £1 shares and 50p shares, each share carrying one vote. A resolution was passed to subdivide each £1 share into two 50p shares, thus doubling the votes of that class. Has there been a variation of the class rights of the 50p shares?

A   Yes, because the voting rights attached to the 50p shares have been affected

B   Yes, because other shares have been created that have the same nominal value and voting rights as the 50p shares

C   No, because the 50p shares still carry one vote per share

D   No, because rights attaching to a class of ordinary shares cannot be varied

Sample Paper LO 2d

---

7   Are the following statements true or false?

A company's 'called up share capital' is so much of the share capital as equals the aggregate amount of the calls made on its shares plus share capital that is paid up without being called and share capital to be paid at a specified future date under the articles or terms of allotment of the relevant shares.

A   True

B   False

A company does not need to issue all its share capital.

C   True

D   False   LO 2d

8   How is authority to allot shares required to be given to the directors of a public limited company?

(1) By ordinary resolution

(2) By special resolution

(3) By the articles of association

A   (1) or (3) only

B   (2) or (3) only

C   (3) only

D   (2) only   LO 2d

---

9   Wayfar Ltd is a private company limited by shares and it has only one class of shares (ordinary shares). Its articles of association give no specific authority for the allotment of shares.

Are the directors empowered to allot ordinary shares of the company in the absence of any members' resolution?

A   Yes

B   No

In the event that the directors make a lawful allotment but fail to register it, are they guilty of an offence?

C   Yes

D   No   LO 2d

---

10 Are the following statements true or false?

A bonus issue is the issue of additional shares, typically fully paid up, to existing shareholders in proportion to their holdings.

A   True

B   False

By making a rights issue, a company requires existing shareholders to subscribe for additional shares in proportion to their holdings.

C   True

D   False   LO 2d

---

11 In which of the following cases, do statutory rights of pre-emption apply?

(1) The allotment of equity securities for cash

(2) The issue of bonus shares

(3) The allotment of equity securities otherwise than for cash

(4) The allotment of securities in relation to an employees' shares scheme

A   (1) only

B   (3) only

C   (2) and (4) only

D   All of the above   LO 2d

12   As a general rule, is a company able to allot shares:

At a premium?

A   Yes

B   No

At a discount?

C   Yes

D   No   LO 2d

13   Joshua and Naomi plan to set up Indigo Ltd, a private company limited by shares. They have some concerns over the payment for shares and ask you whether the following are true:

The shares taken by the company's original subscribers must be paid for in cash.

A   True

B   False

Any shares subsequently allotted must be paid up at least as to one-quarter of the nominal value together with the whole of any share premium payable in respect of them.

C   True

D   False   LO 2d

14   Adam wishes to purchase 100 shares with a nominal value of £1 each in Lovages plc. By way of payment for those shares, can he:

Agree to act as the company's legal adviser for a period of three years?

A   Yes

B   No

Pay 20p per share now, with the remaining 80p per share to be paid at a later date?

C   Yes

D   No   LO 2d

15   Are the following statements true or false?

Shares in a company are freely transferable subject to any restrictions contained in the articles of association.

A   True

B   False

Where a member's shares are transferred, by operation of law, to their trustee in bankruptcy or to their personal representative (as the case may be), there is no requirement for a new share certificate to be prepared.

C   True

D   False   LO 2g

16   In relation to the transfer of shares by electronic means:

Does the CREST transfer system operate in respect of all shares?

A   Yes

B   No

Are companies obliged to permit paperless transfers of shares?

C   Yes

D   No   LO 2g

17   Unico Ltd is a private company limited by shares with 100 shares of 50p each and 100 shares of £1 each. Is Unico Ltd able to:

Subdivide each of its £1 shares into 10 10p shares?

A   Yes

B   No

Consolidate pairs of 50p shares into £1 shares?

C   Yes

D   No   LO 2f

18   In the absence of a court order which directs otherwise, in what circumstances must a public limited company re-register as a private company as a result of a reduction in its share capital?

A   When the directors are unable to issue a solvency statement in respect of the company's liabilities

B   When the company's net assets fall below half of its called up share capital

C   When 20% or more of the company's creditors object to the reduction

D   When the nominal value of the allotted share capital falls below the authorised minimum

                                                                                               LO 2f

19   Zipper Ltd has 100 shares, each with a nominal value of £30 and £3 unpaid. Following an alteration of Zipper Ltd's share capital, the company now has 10,000 shares, each with a nominal value of 30 pence with 27 pence paid up. Which of the following describes the alteration in share capital?

A   Consolidation

B   Subdivision

C   Redenomination

D   Increase in share capital   LO 2f

20 According to the rules on redemption of shares, are the following statements true or false?

In order for a private limited company to issue redeemable shares, the company's articles of association must contain the relevant authority.

A   True

B   False

Redeemable shares may only be issued where there are other shares issued that are not redeemable.

C   True

D   False   LO 2f

21 Are the following statements true or false?

When shares in a limited company are redeemed, they are treated as cancelled and the amount of the company's issued share capital is diminished by the amount of the redemption payment.

A   True

B   False

A company must file notice of redemption and a statement of capital with the Registrar of Companies within one month following a redemption of shares.

C   True

D   False   LO 2f

22 Which of the following describes circumstances where a company may be permitted to acquire some of its own shares provided the transactions are otherwise lawful?

(1) In a reduction of capital

(2) In a redemption of shares

(3) In compliance with a court order

A   All of the above

B   (1) and (2) only

C   (3) only

D   None of the above   LO 2f

23 Rugs plc has recently purchased 500 of its own shares with funds which comprised part of the company's distributable profits. The shares have been cancelled and the company's issued share capital has reduced by £1,000, which amount has been transferred to the company's capital redemption reserve. Are the following statements true or false?

The capital redemption reserve of Rugs plc is treated as part of the company's paid up share capital.

A   True

B   False

The capital redemption reserve of Rugs plc may not be used to pay up new shares which are allotted to members as fully paid bonus shares.

C   True

D   False   LO 2f

24 In which of the following situations may a public limited company lawfully offer financial assistance for the purchase of its shares (provided its net assets are not thereby reduced)?

(1) Where the company lends money as part of its ordinary business

(2) Where the company lends money to a director without a service contract in good faith to enable them to acquire fully paid shares in the company

(3) Where the company gives assistance in the interests of the company for the purposes of an employees' share scheme

A   (1) and (2) only

B   (1) and (3) only

C   (2) and (3) only

D   All of the above   LO 2f

25 Which of the following best defines a debenture?

A   A charge over a company's goodwill

B   The registration document used to register a fixed or floating charge

C   A document that records the terms of any loan

D   A document that records the terms of any secured loan   LO 2n

26 A charge may be avoided by a liquidator as a preference where it is created within a specified time before a company becoming insolvent.

What is the specified time for a fixed charge?

A   6 months

B   9 months

What is the specified time for a floating charge?

C   9 months

D   12 months   LO 2n

27   Are the following statements true or false?

A floating charge created over the 'undertaking and assets' of a company applies only to current assets at the time of the charge.

A   True

B   False

A floating charge is converted into a fixed charge upon crystallisation.

C   True

D   False   LO 2n

28   Bright Bank Ltd has a floating charge over ALL the undertaking and assets of Gateway Ltd. The floating charge contains no provision concerning the subsequent creation of fixed charges. When the charge crystallises Gateway Ltd has the following creditors:

(1)   Giant Bank Ltd, which has a fixed charge over some of Gateway Ltd's assets

(2)   The employees of Gateway Ltd, who are owed remuneration and holiday pay as preferential debts

Do either or both of Giant Bank Ltd and the employees of Gateway Ltd take priority over the charge in favour of Bright Bank Ltd that is now a fixed charge following crystallisation?

A   Giant Bank Ltd only takes priority

B   The employees only take priority

C   Neither take priority

D   Both take priority   LO 2n

29   Every charge entered into by a company has to be registered. Within how many days must registration take place, beginning on the day after the charge is created?

A   7 days

B   14 days

C   21 days

D   28 days   LO 2n

30   Melanie is the company secretary of Swansong Ltd and seeks your advice. She has failed to register a charge entered into by Swansong Ltd within the prescribed period laid down by the Companies Act 2006 and wants to know whether the charge is still valid. What is your advice?

A   The charge is void against any liquidator or administrator but not the chargee or any other creditor

B   The charge remains valid but Swansong Ltd is liable to a fine

C   The charge remains valid but the chargeholder has the option of demanding immediate repayment

D   The charge is void against any liquidator, administrator or creditor   LO 2n

31 A characteristic of a floating charge is that:

It is a charge over a class of assets present and future.

A   Yes

B   No

It is a charge over a class of assets, which, in the ordinary course of the business of the company, will change.

C   Yes

D   No   Sample Paper LO 2n

32 Rules in relation to the issue of shares at premium include:

A company may not, without the authority of its articles, issue its shares at a premium.

A   Yes

B   No

Shares can be issued at a premium not only for cash but also for consideration other than cash.

C   Yes

D   No   LO 2d

33 Sarah wants to sell her shareholding in Albatross plc. Which of the following is correct?

A   If Sarah sold her shares to a person of whom Albatross plc disapproved of it could, without providing any reason, refuse to register the share transfer

B   Sarah will be able to sell her shares through a recognised stock exchange provided they have been listed

C   Sarah must offer to sell her shares to the company before she can offer to sell them to any other person

D   Sarah will not be able to sell her shares unless she can, within three days of any agreement to sell being concluded, produce a printed share certificate as evidence of her title to the shares

Sample Paper LO 2g

Chapter 8: Insolvency law: corporate and personal

1   The aim of administration is described by way of a primary objective and, in the event that the primary objective is not reasonably practicable, a secondary objective, and in the event that this is also not reasonably practicable, an application for an administration will only be successful where a third objective is likely to be satisfied. These **three** objectives are as follows:

   (1)   To realise the company's assets to make a distribution to one or more preferential or secured creditors, without unnecessarily harming the interests of the creditors as a whole

   (2)   To rescue the company in whole or in part as a going concern

   (3)   To achieve a better result for the company's creditors as a whole, than would be likely if the company were wound-up without first going into administration

   In which order are these stated (so that the primary objective is first, followed by the second and third objectives)?

   A   (1), (3), (2)

   B   (2), (1), (3)

   C   (3), (2), (1)

   D   (2), (3), (1)   LO 2o

2   Frazer has a 60% shareholding in Wombles Ltd. He believes that the company should be put into administration, but the other two shareholders, who each own 20%, disagree. Does Frazer have sufficient voting power to be able to pass a resolution that an application to the court should be made for the appointment of an administrator?

   A   Yes

   B   No

   Will he need to satisfy the court that the company is, or is likely to become, unable to pay its debts and that an administration order is reasonably likely to achieve the purpose of administration?

   C   Yes

   D   No   LO 2o

3   Moneylenders plc is a qualifying floating charge holder in respect of Dimble Ltd. After a disastrous three months' trading, Dimble Ltd is placed into liquidation.

   Can Moneylenders plc make a court application for the appointment of an administrator, notwithstanding Dimble Ltd being in liquidation?

   A   Yes

   B   No

   Can Moneylenders plc appoint an administrator out of court?

   C   Yes

   D   No   LO 2o

4   Alan has been appointed administrator of Desktop Ltd. He wishes to obtain statements from a number of the company's officers and employees.

Within how many days must he make his requirements for statements known to them?

A   7 days

B   14 days

How many days do the officers and employees have to comply with his request?

C   11 days

D   21 days   LO 2o

5   Are the following statements true or false?

An administrator's appointment is terminated one year after their appointment unless that period is extended, which can only be done by the court.

A   True

B   False

If the creditors reject the administrator's proposals, the court may make any order it sees fit, including terminating the administrator's appointment.

C   True

D   False   LO 2o

6   With regard to the powers of an administrator, are they empowered to:

Remove a director?

A   Yes

B   No

Make payments to unsecured creditors?

C   Yes

D   No   LO 2o

7   With regard to the powers of an administrator, are they entitled to:

Present a petition for the winding up of the company?

A   Yes

B   No

Remove one director and replace them by appointing another person?

C   Yes

D   No   LO 2o

8   Benchline Ltd has been placed in administration, following an application by one of its floating charge holders. Little Bank Ltd has a fixed charge over one of the retail premises of Benchline Ltd.

Can the members of Benchline Ltd pass a resolution for the voluntary winding up of the company?

A   Yes

B   No

Is Little Bank Ltd entitled to enforce its fixed charge without obtaining the consent of the administrator or the court?

C   Yes

D   No   LO 2o

9   Morphitts plc has been placed in administration. Nymph Ltd is owed £100,000 and is worried that if Morphitts plc ends up in liquidation, the debt will be irrecoverable.

Is Nymph Ltd able to pursue recovery of the debt due from Morphitts plc?

A   Yes

B   No

Can Nymph Ltd petition the court for the winding up of Morphitts plc?

C   Yes

D   No   LO 2o

10 In respect of a company in administration, are the following statements true or false?

A creditor or member can apply to the court if they feel that the administrator has acted in a way that has harmed their interest.

A   True

B   False

The employees of the company are automatically dismissed on the appointment of an administrator.

C   True

D   False   LO 2o

11 What is the primary role of a receiver?

A   To rescue the company as a going concern

B   To realise the charged assets and pay off the appointing chargeholder's debt

C   To pay off creditors with preferential rights

D   To manage the company pending the appointment of an administrator or liquidator   LO 2o

12 Who is entitled to propose a company voluntary arrangement?

(1) The directors
(2) An administrator
(3) A liquidator

A   (1) only

B   (2) or (3) only

C   None of the above

D   All of the above   LO 2o

13 Are the following statements true or false?

Once approved, a company voluntary arrangement becomes binding on all creditors.

A   True

B   False

A company voluntary arrangement typically lasts for 6 to 12 months.

C   True

D   False   LO 2o

14 With regard to a members' voluntary winding up of a company:

The declaration of solvency is to be made by:

A   the directors, acting unanimously

B   a majority of the directors

In appointing a liquidator, the company must pass:

C   an ordinary resolution

D   a special resolution   LO 2o

15 Are the following statements true or false?

Creditors play no part in a members' voluntary liquidation.

A   True

B   False

The declaration of solvency applicable to a members' voluntary winding up must be made not more than five weeks before the resolution to wind up is passed.

C   True

D   False   LO 2o

16 The members of Recycle Ltd resolve to wind up the company. Since it is not possible to make a declaration of solvency, a creditors' meeting is called. At that meeting, who may appoint a liquidator?

(1) The members

(2) The creditors

A (1) only

B (2) only

C Both (1) and (2)

D Neither (1) nor (2) LO 2o

17 Darren is owed £25,000 by Innovations Ltd. He proposes to petition the court for a compulsory winding up of the company, on the grounds that it is insolvent. He seeks your advice.

Since Darren is owed more than £750, can he submit a petition to court immediately?

A Yes

B No

Must Darren provide additional evidence to satisfy the court that Innovations Ltd is unable to pay its debts or that its assets are less than its liabilities?

C Yes

D No LO 2o

18 Are the following statements true or false?

A petition to wind up a company on the grounds that it is just and equitable to do so, will only be made where the court is satisfied that the company is unable, or is likely to become unable, to pay its debts.

A True

B False

A member who petitions the court on the grounds that it is just and equitable to do so must, generally speaking, have been registered as a shareholder for at least six months out of the last 18 months before the petition being presented.

C True

D False LO 2o

19 On a compulsory winding up of a company, who will the court usually appoint?

A The secured creditor owed the greatest amount of money by the company

B The auditor of the company

C The Official Receiver

D A qualified insolvency practitioner LO 2o

20 Lionel is appointed liquidator of Laburnum Ltd.

Do the company's assets automatically vest in Lionel?

A   Yes

B   No

Are the employees of Laburnum Ltd automatically dismissed when Lionel is appointed as liquidator?

C   Yes

D   No   LO 2o

21 Fernline plc is in liquidation and Gerald is the liquidator. He has discovered that Fernline plc sold one of its principal offices for significantly less than its market value 18 months ago. It is quite clear that the directors knew that the company was heading for insolvency when it agreed the sale.

Is the sale of the office a transaction at an undervalue that is liable to be avoided by Gerald within the provisions of the Insolvency Act 1986?

A   Yes

B   No

Where a liquidator can avoid a transaction at an undervalue, can they order the return of the property in order to restore the position to what it would have been if no such transaction had taken place?

C   Yes

D   No   LO 2o

22 Malcolm has just been appointed liquidator of Tenpin Ltd. The company entered into a floating charge in favour of one of its directors, Duncan, 13 months ago.

Might the floating charge be void as against Malcolm?

A   Yes

B   No

Would it be possible for Malcolm, as liquidator, to institute proceedings against Duncan, for wrongful trading or fraudulent trading, in an attempt to make him personally liable for some or all of the company's debts?

C   Yes

D   No   LO 2o

23 In distributing a company's assets in a compulsory liquidation, in which order will the following receive any payments due to them?

(1) Floating chargees

(2) Members

(3) Employees who are owed accrued holiday pay

A   (1), (2), (3)

B   (2), (3), (1)

C   (3), (1), (2)

D   (3), (2), (1)

LO 2p

24 Smallchange Ltd is in compulsory liquidation and the liquidator has realised a fund of £7,600 available for distribution. The costs of the liquidation (including remuneration of the liquidator) amount to £2,300. There is a floating charge of £4,000. Employees are owed accrued holiday pay of £1,200. Marcus is owed £500 by the company but he has no security.

Do the 'ring-fencing' provisions apply in favour of unsecured creditors?

A   Yes

B   No

Will Marcus be paid in full?

C   Yes

D   No

LO 2p

25 What percentage of creditors is required to approve a proposed individual voluntary arrangement (IVA) at a creditors' meeting convened for that purpose?

A   Over 50%

B   75%

C   90%

D   95%

LO 2p

26 Who **may** petition for bankruptcy?

(1) The individual debtor

(2) Any creditor of that debtor who is owed at least £750

(3) A supervisor of an approved individual voluntary arrangement (IVA) in respect of that debtor

A   (1) and (2) only

B   (2) and (3) only

C   (1) or (3)

D   (1), (2) or (3)

LO 2p

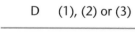

27 Demelza had always been successful in business until twelve months ago. After a competitor moved in to adjoining premises, however, her business suffered and she became increasingly depressed by her rising debts. She petitioned for bankruptcy. The total unsecured debts owed amount to £39,000 and the value of her bankruptcy estate is likely to be around £6,000–£7,000.

Is the court likely to make a bankruptcy order in respect of Demelza?

A   Yes

B   No

Would your answer be different if one of Demelza's creditors had petitioned for her bankruptcy?

C   Yes

D   No   LO 2p

28 Are the following statements true or false?

Where there is insufficient money in a bankrupt's estate to satisfy all unsecured creditors, the debts are discharged according to the date on which they were incurred.

A   True

B   False

The Official Receiver (or other insolvency practitioner) must act to maximise funds available to satisfy the individual debtor's creditors.

C   True

D   False   LO 2p

29 Once a bankruptcy order has been made:

Can a secured creditor enforce their security against the bankrupt debtor?

A   Yes

B   No

Does the debtor's property vest in the trustee in bankruptcy?

C   Yes

D   No   LO 2p

30 John is a self-employed decorator who has just been declared bankrupt. He has recently agreed to sell his car to his neighbour.

In calculating the total value of John's estate, will his decorating tools be included?

A   Yes

B   No

Can John go ahead and sell his car?

C   Yes

D   No   LO 2p

31   Jemima is a trustee in bankruptcy in respect of Craig's bankruptcy. In which order will the following receive payment out of the Craig's estate of any sums payable to them?

(1)   Craig

(2)   The liquidator (in respect of his remuneration and expenses)

(3)   Craig's wife (whom he owed £200)

A   (1), (2), (3)

B   (2), (3), (1)

C   (3), (1), (2)

D   (3), (2), (1)

LO 2p

32   Under Schedule B1 of the Insolvency Act 1986 one or more of a set of three objectives have to be met in order for the application for an administration order to be successful.

Do the following statements represent one of these objectives?

To put a rescue plan into place if it is possible to rescue the company in whole or in part as a going concern.

A   Yes

B   No

If corporate rescue is not possible, to maximise returns to creditors over and above what would be achieved had the company not gone into administration first.

C   Yes

D   No

Sample Paper LO 2o

33   Under the Insolvency Act 1986 a petition to have a company compulsorily wound up is likely to be successful:

Where there has been a fraud on the minority.

A   Yes

B   No

Where the court is of the opinion that it is just and equitable that the company should be wound-up.

C   Yes

D   No

Sample Paper LO 2o

34   In the event of liquidation the liquidator will distribute the assets of the company concerned to creditors in accordance with the priority determined by the law relating to insolvency. Assuming there are surplus assets, which of the following creditors will the liquidator repay **last**?

A   Preferential debts

B   Fixed chargeholders

C   Return of contributed capital to ordinary shareholders

D   Floating chargeholders

Sample Paper LO 2p

Chapter 9: Sole traders and partnerships

1 Damian, Isabella and Sean decide to go into business together selling a complete gardening service, from landscape design to adding garden ornaments. They call the business Damian & Co. They each invest £3,000 and agree to share profits equally. After two years, they have made a loss of £950 and no longer believe the venture to be viable. Which of the following statements best describes their business organisation?

    A   It is not an ordinary partnership because it is called Damian & Co

    B   It is an ordinary partnership because they agree to invest and share profits equally

    C   It is not an ordinary partnership because they have not entered into a written partnership agreement

    D   It is an ordinary partnership because they are in business together and intend to make a profit even though they make a loss

                             LO 2a

---

2 Are the following statements true or false?

An ordinary partnership is a separate legal entity from its partners.

    A   True

    B   False

The Partnership Act 1890 governs the rights and duties of partners in an ordinary partnership, in the absence of an express provision to the contrary.

    C   True

    D   False

                             LO 2a

---

3 Mark and Liam are in partnership together, running a coffee shop. They have not entered into a formal partnership agreement but have agreed to share profits on the basis of two-thirds to Mark and one-third to Liam. Are the following statements true or false?

If the partnership makes a loss, this will be borne equally by Mark and Liam.

    A   True

    B   False

Both Mark and Liam are entitled to appoint a new partner, without obtaining each other's consent.

    C   True

    D   False

                             LO 2a

4   Humphreys & Co is a partnership involved in the sale of hot tubs. Due to a summer of rotten weather, the business fails and the partnership is dissolved. Are the following statements true or false?

Any partner (whatever his share of profits) can insist on the partnership assets being realised and any surplus being distributed (after payment of debts) to the partners.

A   True

B   False

In the event of there being a capital deficiency, the remaining partners of the firm will bear the loss equally in the absence of an express agreement to the contrary.

C   True

D   False   LO 2a

5   Lola and May are in partnership. Their business, Lomays & Co, buys gift products made by local craftsmen and sells them through well-known retail outlets. Lola sometimes receives a commission from the suppliers, supposedly for Lomays & Co,when she places an order for a large number of products. She rarely informs May of the commission nor does she pay the commission into the firm's bank account. Lola, to May's knowledge, also purchases homemade cards from Original Greetings Ltd, a company that she owns and runs with another friend, and sells them along with other items through the Lomays business. Which of the following best describes the legal position, in view of the fiduciary duties owed by partners?

A   May is entitled to buy out Lola's share of the business

B   Lola must account to Lomays & Co for commission monies received

C   Lola must account to Lomays & Co for commissions received and profits made by Original Greetings Ltd on cards sold through Lomays & Co

D   Lola must account for commission monies received and must refrain from selling products of Original Greetings Ltd through Lomays & Co because of the obvious conflict of interest
                                                                                                 LO 2a

6   Freda, Gaynor and Hank are in partnership as solicitors. Freda and Gaynor authorise Hank to appoint a junior solicitor to work in the conveyancing department. Accordingly, Hank appoints Jane but since Hank is overworked in the commercial department, he also appoints John, another junior solicitor, to help him in the commercial department. Which of the following statements best describes whether Freda, Gaynor and the firm are bound by the appointment of John?

A   Freda, Gaynor and the firm are bound because the appointment is within the usual authority of a partner

B   They are not bound because Hank has exceeded his authority, which was to appoint a junior solicitor for the conveyancing department

C   They are bound because John knew that Hank was a partner in the firm

D   They are bound because John did not know that Hank did not have express authority to appoint him   LO 1e

7   Matt, Gemma and James are in partnership running a business organising conferences. Gemma and James nominate Matt to advertise their business and they all agree a total budget of £3,000 for this purpose. Matt feels that they should advertise in some glossy magazines as well as newspapers but knows that Gemma and James will not agree. Nevertheless, Matt places an advertisement with Upmarket Businesses, a high quality monthly glossy magazine. This incurs an additional cost of £2,000 (resulting in a total cost of £5,000), to be paid within 30 days. When Gemma and James hear about it, they are angry that Matt has exceeded the authority that they gave him and refuse to pay the publisher of Upmarket Businesses for the advertisement. Which of the following best describes whether Upmarket Businesses can enforce the contract?

    A   No. Matt had no authority to enter into the contract

    B   Yes. Matt had implied usual authority to advertise the firm's business

    C   Yes. Matt had no authority but Upmarket Businesses was not aware of that fact

    D   Yes. Matt had no authority but Upmarket Businesses was not aware of that fact but knew that he was a partner

                                                                                                    LO 1e

8   Mark, Nathan and Oliver are in partnership together running a cattle market, under the name Cattle Galore & Co. Mark enters into a contract, using the firm's headed writing paper, to purchase 10 bulls from Farmer Giles for the firm. When Nathan and Oliver hear about it they refuse to honour the contract because they had all agreed at the previous partnership meeting, that they would not purchase any more livestock for the next six months due to the firm's financial situation. Mark insists that the contract was too good an opportunity to miss. Which of the following best describes the legal position?

    A   Mark alone is liable on the contract because he acted without the other partners' authority

    B   Mark, Nathan and Oliver are personally liable, since partners are agents of each other

    C   Cattle Galore & Co is liable as it was a contract entered into for the purposes of the partnership business

    D   The firm and, therefore, all of its partners are liable on the contract to purchase 10 bulls from Farmer Giles

                                                                                                    LO 1e

9   Chad, Digby and Elliott are partners in the Bespoke Catering Co. Elliott joined the firm on 1 June. On 10 May, the firm had entered into a contract for the purchase of a new delivery van but is now refusing to take delivery of it. Which of the following best describes the legal position?

    A   Elliott is liable because every partner is liable for the firm's contractual commitments

    B   Elliott is not liable because the contract was entered into before he became a partner

    C   Elliott is liable because the law implies that on joining the partnership a partner assumes liability on existing debts unless there is a specific agreement to the contrary

    D   Elliott is not liable because the firm that entered into the contract was dissolved and re-formed when Elliott became a partner

                                                                                                    LO 1e, 2a

10 Are the following statements true or false?

An ordinary partnership may only be dissolved by the unanimous consent of the partners.

A   True

B   False

Where a partnership becomes insolvent, bankruptcy proceedings can be brought in respect of individual partners.

C   True

D   False   LO 2a

11 Pascal and his son Roger are partners in the firm, Smith & Co. After a disastrous year, they have realised that they cannot settle all the debts owed by the partnership. One creditor, with a fixed charge over the main business premises, now wishes to enforce his security.

Can the secured creditor take action against Pascal and Roger individually or sue them in the name of Smith & Co?

A   Yes

B   No

Can the partnership be wound up?

C   Yes

D   No   LO 2a

12 In relation to ordinary partnerships, answer the following.

Can the partnership raise finance by creating a floating charge over its assets or undertaking?

A   Yes

B   No

Can a partner assign their interest in the partnership to another person?

C   Yes

D   No   LO 2a

13 Are the following statements true or false in relation to ordinary partnerships?

A partner is not entitled to assign their interest in the partnership.

A   True

B   False

The liability of a partner is unlimited.

C   True

D   False   LO 2a

14 Are the following statements true or false in relation to a limited liability partnership (LLP)?

An LLP has a legal personality distinct from its members.

A   True

B   False

An LLP must have at least one member whose liability is unlimited.

C   True

D   False   LO 2c

15 Blodwin and his partner Theo want to set up a limited liability partnership (LLP) as they understand that it offers a number of advantages over an ordinary partnership. They ask you the following questions:

Will the LLP be liable to tax along the same lines as a registered company?

A   Yes

B   No

Will they need to disclose their names and addresses when they apply for registration?

C   Yes

D   No   LO 2b, 2c

16 Ashad and Michael plan to set up a limited liability partnership (LLP) to continue the business, Jenkins & Co, that they have conducted for the past 15 years as an ordinary partnership.

They particularly do not want to change the name because it is a successful business. Can they register the LLP under the name Jenkins & Co?

A   Yes

B   No

Do they need to have a formal partnership agreement?

C   Yes

D   No   LO 2b, 2c

17 Janet and Carol have, helped by their solicitor, drawn up a formal partnership agreement for their new partnership, Bloomin Flowers LLP. They would like answers to the following questions.

Can they file their partnership agreement as a means of applying to register their LLP, since it contains all the information required on incorporation?

A   Yes

B   No

When their business is up and running, will they need to submit confirmation statements to the Registrar of Companies?

C   Yes

D   No   LO 2b, 2c

18 Arthur, Peter and William are members of Money Matters LLP. Which of the following statements is incorrect (assuming no other express provisions in the agreement are relevant)?

A Arthur, Peter and William each have the right to take part in the management of the partnership business

B Arthur, Peter and William are each entitled to receive remuneration in respect of the part they each play in the business

C Arthur can give reasonable notice to the other partners that he intends to cease to be a member

D A change in the membership of an LLP must be notified to the Registrar of Companies within 14 days

LO 2j

19 Are the following statements true or false in relation to a limited liability partnership (LLP)?

A member of an LLP is an agent of the LLP as well as its members.

A True

B False

A member cannot bind the LLP by their actions unless they act within their actual express or implied authority.

C True

D False

LO 2c, 2j

20 The business of Lush-Limos LLP has suffered badly from fewer people having extravagant weddings due to a recession and is now in a position where it is unable to meet its debts. Of the following possible options that are relevant to an insolvent company, which are applicable to a limited liability partnership?

(1) Voluntary arrangement

(2) Administration

(3) Voluntary liquidation

(4) Compulsory liquidation

A All of them

B (2) and (4) only

C (3) and (4) only

D (2), (3) and (4) only

LO 2c

21 Max and Lily were members in an limited liability partnership (LLP) and, in accordance with their partnership agreement, could withdraw £20,000 per annum each. Max and Lily both withdrew £20,000 in each of the past two years, even though it was clear 15 months ago that the LLP was going to become insolvent. Which of the following best describes the legal position?

    A   Max and Lily have no liability because they acted in accordance with the partnership agreement

    B   The withdrawals made in the last 12 months can be clawed back on the grounds that the members had reasonable grounds to believe that the LLP would become insolvent

    C   Withdrawals made in the last two years can be clawed back if it can be shown that, at the time of making each withdrawal, Max and Lily had reasonable grounds to believe that the LLP would become insolvent

    D   Both withdrawals can be clawed back, regardless of their knowledge or belief at the time, because the LLP has since become insolvent   LO 2c

22 Do each of the following statements represent a statutory right for a partner of a firm under the Partnership Act 1890?

To share in the capital, profits and losses of the business in proportion to their initial capital contribution to the firm.

    A   Yes

    B   No

To have unfettered access to the firm's books.

    C   Yes

    D   No   Sample Paper LO 1e

23 Under the Limited Liability Partnerships Act 2000 certain requirements need to be met for a limited liability partnership (LLP) to be legitimately formed. Are the following among those requirements?

One or more persons who are associated for the purposes of carrying on a lawful business with a view to a profit must have subscribed their names to an incorporation document.

    A   Yes

    B   No

The incorporation document must state the name of the LLP which must end with the words 'Limited Liability Partnership' or the abbreviation 'LLP'.

    C   Yes

    D   No   Sample Paper LO 2b

24 Under the Limited Liability Partnership Regulations 2001, and in the absence of contrary provision, the rights of members of a limited liability partnership include the right to:

Remuneration for acting in the business or management of the limited liability partnership

A   Yes

B   No

Share equally in the profits of the limited liability partnership

C   Yes

D   No   Sample Paper LO 2j

25 Are the following statements concerning sole traders true or false?

Before commencing business, a sole trader must obtain a licence and register for VAT.

A   True

B   False

All business profits accrue to the sole trader.

C   True

D   False   LO 2a

26 Which of the following statements concerning sole traders is correct?

A   A sole trader must file simplified accounts with the Registrar each year

B   A sole trader must appoint an auditor if the business's size meets the same criteria as medium-sized companies

C   A sole trader must report the business's finances to the tax authorities each year

D   A sole trader's business is legally distinct from their personal wealth   LO 2a

Chapter 10: Criminal law

1 In order to receive the protection conferred by the whistleblowing provisions of the Public Interest Disclosure Act 1998:

Does a person need to be an 'employee'?

A Yes

B No

Does the person need to be of a minimum age?

C Yes

D No   LO 3a

2 Sam has been working in his employer's factory for five months. He plans to make public some information about his employer's unsafe working practices, but he has been told the following things about the protection afforded by the whistleblowing provisions contained in the Public Interest Disclosure Act 1998. Are they true or false?

That statutory protection is not available to Sam because he has less than one year's continuous service with his employer.

A True

B False

That he will have to prove that his employer's working practices are unsafe.

C True

D False   LO 3a

3 Which of the following criteria does a person not always have to show in order to receive the protection offered by statute in a case of whistleblowing?

A That the disclosure is a qualifying disclosure

B That it is made with a reasonable belief in its truth

C That they have some documentary evidence of the matter complained of

D That it has been made to an appropriate person or recognised regulatory body   LO 3a

4 Which of the following disclosures is or are qualifying disclosure(s)?

(1) That a criminal offence is likely to be committed

(2) That their employer has been guilty of negligence

(3) That the work of their employer is causing damage to the environment

(4) That their employer is engaging in unsafe working practices

A (1) and (4) only

B (1), (3) and (4) only

C All of the above

D (3) and (4) only   LO 3a

5   The Public Interest Disclosure Act 1998 protects workers who make a qualifying disclosure in relation to their employer's activities. Are the following statements true or false?

It is sufficient that the worker making the disclosure to the appropriate regulatory body (eg, the Health and Safety Executive in health and safety cases) holds a reasonable belief that the information they are disclosing is correct.

A   True

B   False

Disclosure of information by a worker to the Environment Agency, which shows a cover-up by their employer of damage that the employer has caused to the environment, may constitute a qualifying disclosure.

C   True

D   False   LO 3a

6   Raj worked as a junior administrator in the offices of an insurance company Be Sure & Co. He had been hoping to be promoted to a senior post recently but his colleague was given the job, even though he was younger than Raj and had not worked in the office as long as Raj had. Raj has also discovered that his boss was paying the staff in the post room less than the minimum wage. Still angry about missing out on his promotion, he has passed this information on to the senior partner of Be Sure & Co. Are the following true or false?

The disclosure is a qualifying disclosure under the Public Interest Disclosure Act 1998 because it reveals non-compliance with a legal obligation to which the employer is subject.

A   True

B   False

The disclosure is not protected under the Public Interest Disclosure Act 1998 because the motive behind it shows a lack of good faith.

C   True

D   False   LO 3a

7   Nina is a nurse working in the National Health Service. She has seen Mike, an NHS consultant for whom she often works, stealing medicinal drugs from the hospital supplies on three occasions in the last month. Mike knows that she has seen him but believes that she would never divulge the information to anybody. Are the following statements true or false?

Nina must disclose Mike's wrongdoing either internally within the NHS or to a legal adviser, in order to receive the protection afforded by the Public Interest Disclosure Act 1998.

A   True

B   False

If, as a result of her disclosing what she knows, Nina is denied a promotion, she will be entitled to compensation.

C   True

D   False   LO 3a

8   The Public Interest Disclosure Act 1998 protects workers who make a qualifying disclosure in relation to their employer's activities. Are the following statements true or false?

In order to gain the protection of the 1998 Act, a worker must make a qualifying disclosure internally in the first instance.

A   True

B   False

A qualifying disclosure to a legal adviser must be made in the course of obtaining legal advice.

C   True

D   False   LO 3a

9   Martin proposes to disclose information to the police about his employer's criminal acts but he has been told that he will need to satisfy certain criteria in order for such a disclosure to be protected by the Public Interest Disclosure Act 1998. For instance:

Does it matter if Martin's proposed disclosure is made, principally, for personal gain?

A   Yes

B   No

Does Martin need to have raised the matter already internally or with a prescribed regulator?

C   Yes

D   No   LO 3a

10   With regard to the offence of fraud under the Fraud Act 2006, is it necessary to show that the defendant intended to make a gain for themselves or another person?

A   Yes

B   No

If a director of a company is found guilty of fraudulent trading, will they automatically be disqualified from acting as a director?

C   Yes

D   No   LO 3b

11   Jack has been convicted of fraud under the Fraud Act 2006. What is the maximum sanction that can be imposed on him?

A   7 years' imprisonment and an unlimited fine

B   10 years' imprisonment and a fine of up to £100,000

C   7 years' imprisonment and a fine of up to £100,000

D   10 years' imprisonment and an unlimited fine   LO 3b

12 With regard to the criminal offence of fraudulent trading, answer the following:

Can this offence be committed by a director of a company even if the company is not in liquidation?

A   Yes

B   No

Is this offence committed where a business is carried on for **any** fraudulent purpose?

C   Yes

D   No   LO 3b

13 Danny is a director of Country Living Ltd, and Carol is its company secretary. Danny and Carol have just completed documentation for an order of garden furniture worth £72,000, even though the company has outstanding debts of over £50,000. They have deliberately not told Frank, Country Living Ltd's finance director, and they do not have a clear idea of how the business will be able to pay off the amounts it already owes its creditors. They consider that to be Frank's problem. Which of the following best describes the legal position?

A   Danny might be guilty of fraudulent trading but Carol will not be guilty as she is not a director

B   Both Danny and Carol might be guilty of fraudulent trading

C   Neither Danny nor Carol will be guilty of fraudulent trading since the company is not in liquidation

D   Both Danny and Carol are subject to mandatory disqualification in respect of their actions

LO 3b

14 Nigel and Kevin are directors of Go Karts Ltd. Leo, the company's financial adviser, tells Kevin that the company is facing mounting debts and that its assets and projected income is not sufficient to pay them. Notwithstanding this, Kevin orders 20 state-of-the-art go-karts, in the hope that he would be able to keep at least one of the go-karts once the company was wound up (as he knew it would be). Three months later, the company goes into compulsory liquidation. Nigel has never been involved with the day to day running of the company as he is much too busy with his other business ventures. As far as he's concerned, Go Karts Ltd is doing very well. Which of the following best describes who is and who is not guilty of the criminal offence of fraudulent trading?

A   Kevin and Leo are guilty. Nigel is not guilty because he is unaware of the situation

B   Kevin and Nigel are guilty. Leo is not guilty because he is a financial adviser and not a director

C   Kevin is guilty. Leo and Nigel are not guilty because neglect or lack of positive dishonest action cannot constitute fraudulent trading

D   Nigel, Kevin and Leo are all guilty because they are all aware or should be aware that insolvency is likely   LO 3b

15 The Criminal Justice Act 1993 governs the criminal offence of insider dealing. Which of the following best describes the offence of insider dealing?

    A   Making public information relating to price-affected securities in order to influence dealings in those securities

    B   Dealing in securities while in possession of inside information as an insider, the securities being price-affected by the information

    C   Acquiring securities with the benefit of price-sensitive information obtained as an insider

    D   Being an insider and in possession of confidential information about the likely effect of dealings on the price of securities   LO 3b

---

16 Richard is a fund manager with Burrington Fund Managers Ltd. He hears that Ventures plc is about to announce a successful takeover and that its share price will rise significantly as a result. He texts his brother-in-law, Jeff, and says 'If I were you, I'd buy as many shares as you can in Ventures plc'. Jeff has mislaid his mobile phone and doesn't receive the information until after the takeover has been announced.

Is Richard guilty of insider dealing contrary to the Criminal Justice Act 1993?

    A   Yes

    B   No

Would it make any difference if Jeff bought shares in Ventures plc?

    C   Yes

    D   No   LO 3b

---

17 Robert is a corporate banker and is just about to close a deal in which Bigfish plc is to take over Smallfry Ltd. He knows that this will mean a huge increase in the share price of Smallfry Ltd. He is chatting to a friend, Freya, over lunch and tells her all about it because it has been an exciting deal. Freya has never dealt in shares and never seems to have any money to spend anyway. However, unknown to Robert, Freya has just inherited £10,000 and immediately goes out and buys shares in Smallfry Ltd.

Is Robert guilty of encouraging another person to deal, contrary to the Criminal Justice Act 1993?

    A   Yes

    B   No

Is Robert guilty of disclosing inside information that he obtained in the course of his employment?

    C   Yes

    D   No   LO 3b

18 Andy is an auditor doing an audit of Sunstar plc. During the course of the audit, he learns that the company has made an unexpected heavy loss in the current financial year. He tells his colleague Zara back in the firm's office and she sells her shares in Sunstar plc.

Is the information passed to Zara inside information for the purposes of the insider dealing provisions of the Criminal Justice Act 1993?

A   Yes

B   No

Is Zara an insider for the purposes of those provisions?

C   Yes

D   No   LO 3b

19 Marcus is auditing the accounts of Zonefest plc. He is aware that the company is about to announce huge profits. He tells Amy what he knows, as he knows that she already owns shares in Zonefest plc. Amy buys a further 100 shares but later says that she had been planning to buy more shares anyway. Marcus also includes the information in a report to his senior partner, Karl, who quickly buys 200 shares in Zonefest plc.

Is Amy guilty of insider dealing, contrary to the Criminal Justice Act 1993?

A   Yes

B   No

Is Marcus guilty of insider dealing, contrary to the Criminal Justice Act 1993 in relation to his report to Karl?

C   Yes

D   No   LO 3b

20 Are the following statements true or false?

Bribery is the criminal offence that is committed by the person who **offers** the money or favour, whereas corruption is the criminal offence that is committed by the person who **receives** the money or favour.

A   True

B   False

The offence of bribery cannot be committed unless the person who is offered money or other favour is in public office.

C   True

D   False   LO 3c

21 Lucy is a UK national who has been living in France for the past three years. She now wishes to return to England and is keen to secure a deal on a very desirable building plot being sold by First Class Homes plc at auction. She knows the managing director of the company and so, keen to avoid attending an auction, she offers him £5,000 in cash (for his personal account) if he will arrange for the company to sell the building plot to her by private agreement, rather than by auction. The director refuses and the property goes to auction where Lucy is outbid by another buyer.

Are the following statements true or false?

Where the person who is offered money refuses it, no offence of bribery is committed.

A   True

B   False

Lucy may be guilty of the offence of bribery.

C   True

D   False   LO 3c

22 Are the following statements true or false?

Bribery is a criminal offence and is governed by statute.

A   True

B   False

The maximum penalty is an unlimited fine and imprisonment for up to seven years.

C   True

D   False   LO 3c

23 Which of the following best describes the offence of money laundering which is governed by the Proceeds of Crime Act 2002?

A   It is the process by which the proceeds of illegal activity are disposed of into apparently legitimate business activities

B   It is the process by which monies are transferred from business to business or place to place in order to conceal their original source

C   It is the process by which property illegally obtained is converted into cash in order to facilitate its disposal

D   It is the process by which the proceeds of crime are converted into assets which appear to have a legitimate origin   LO 3d

24 What is the maximum length of imprisonment that can be imposed under the Proceeds of Crime Act 2002 for failing to report a suspicion of money laundering?

A   5 years

B   7 years

C   10 years

D   14 years   LO 3d

25   Nathan works as an accountant with Moneyneeds Ltd, a financial services company. He is asked to
      prepare some accounts which he strongly suspects are going to be used to enable the company to
      evade some of its tax liability. He makes a report to the MLRO nominated by his employer but, in
      fear of losing his job if he does not do as he is asked, he also prepares the accounts as required.

      Is he guilty of money laundering under the Proceeds of Crime Act 2002?

      A   Yes

      B   No

      Is he guilty of tipping off under the Proceeds of Crime Act 2002?

      C   Yes

      D   No   Sample Paper LO 3d

26   Xavier is an accountant who works as a sole trader. One of his clients is the proprietor of Pony
      Foods Ltd who is keen to reduce his company's tax liability in the coming financial year. He asks
      Xavier for some tax advice which Xavier believes is aimed at evading tax. Which of the following
      best describes the legal position?

      A   Xavier may report his suspicion of money laundering to the National Crime Agency (NCA) but
           will be liable for breach of the duty of confidentiality owed to his client

      B   Xavier should report his suspicion of money laundering to the NCA because he is not bound
           by client confidentiality or excused by legal professional privilege

      C   Xavier is bound by client confidentiality and should not report his suspicions to the NCA

      D   Xavier is under legal professional privilege because his advice is sought on legal matters. He
           should not, therefore, report his suspicions to the NCA   LO 3d

27   James is an accountant in a local accountancy firm and advises Creedy Ltd, the parent company of
      a number of subsidiaries. James notices that a number of transactions taking place between the
      subsidiaries in the group appear to have no explanation or business justification and also that each
      subsidiary is transferring funds to an overseas subsidiary (in a tax haven) with increasing frequency.
      He strongly suspects that the companies are being used to conceal proceeds of criminal activities,
      but he is worried about his duty of client confidentiality. Assuming his suspicions are reasonably
      well founded:

      Should James report his suspicions to the nominated MLRO within his firm?

      A   Yes

      B   No

      Should James tell one of the directors of Creedy Ltd about his suspicions?

      C   Yes

      D   No   LO 3d

28 Gary owns a large estate agency business and has recently become aware that he is required by law to establish some internal systems and procedures designed to prevent the possibility of money laundering. He comes to you for advice in respect of the Money Laundering Regulations 2007 and in particular as to whether the following are true or false.

The appointment of a Money Laundering Reporting Officer is recommended but not compulsory.

A   True

B   False

Failure to implement measures required by the Regulations is punishable by an unlimited fine and up to two years' imprisonment.

C   True

D   False   LO 3d

29 There is no defence to a charge of bribery.

A   True

B   False

Whenever an employee commits an offence of bribery, the commercial organisation for which they work is also guilty of an offence under the Bribery Act 2010 for failing to prevent the commission of the offence.

C   True

D   False   LO 3c

30 Under the Public Interest Disclosure Act 1998 a worker would be required to follow their organisation's internally or externally mandated whistleblowing procedures where they have a reasonable belief that:

A criminal offence is being committed eg, fraud

A   Yes

B   No

The health and safety of their organisation's workers is being put at risk

C   Yes

D   No   Sample Paper LO 3a

31 Under the Companies Act 2006 the maximum penalty that can be given where an officer of a company has been convicted of carrying on their company's business with intent to defraud, may include:

An unlimited fine

A   True

B   False

A period of imprisonment of up to 10 years

C   True

D   False   Sample Paper LO 3b

32 Are the following statements true or false in relation to the provisions relating to fraudulent trading contained in the Companies Act 2006?

They do not apply unless the business was carried on with intent to defraud or for any fraudulent purpose.

A   True

B   False

A successful conviction for fraudulent trading could be secured against an officer of a company who had secured further credit for the company, at a time when they suspected that there was no reasonable prospect of the company being able to repay the debt.

C   True

D   False   Sample Paper LO 3b

33 In relation to the criminal offence of bribery:

Offering a person in public office money or other favours in order to circumvent the ethical guidelines of their professional body is an offence.

A   True

B   False

It is punishable by a term of imprisonment or a fine, or in serious cases both imprisonment and a fine.

C   True

D   False   Sample Paper LO 3c, 3e

34 Brisco LLP, a firm of ICAEW Chartered Accountants, is the auditor of Spelt plc. At a meeting in April with Spelt plc's directors, Abel Brisco, Brisco's senior partner, signed the auditor's report in respect of the financial statements for the year ended 31 January. At that meeting Spelt plc's finance director mentioned a forthcoming takeover bid for a majority of the shares of Spelt plc by Wyman plc, and said that Wyman plc would be using the most recent set of financial statements in fixing a price for the shares of Spelt plc.

A few months later, in October, following its successful takeover bid for Spelt plc, Wyman plc sued Brisco LLP for negligence in auditing Spelt's financial statements which, Wyman plc claimed, significantly overstated the value of revenue. In a private meeting about the case with the Brisco partners, Abel Brisco said that because there had been no written notification of Wyman plc's reliance on the financial statements he would deny having received any verbal notification.

Are the following statements true or false?

Brisco is likely to owe a duty of care to Wyman which was a known bidder, even though the firm had not been informed in writing.

A   True

B   False

Abel Brisco is likely to be in breach of the ICAEW Code of Ethics in respect of professional behaviour.

C   True

D   False   LO 3e

35 Gavin, a partner in Ingatestone & Co, is the engagement partner on the audit of Tolleshunt Electronics Ltd (Tolleshunt). He is in a close personal relationship with the finance director of Tolleshunt, and agrees to sign an unmodified audit report on the company's accounts despite its having declared a dividend which is illegal under the Companies Act 2006. The finance director has a substantial personal shareholding in Tolleshunt.

Is Gavin in breach of:

The Proceeds of Crime Act 2002 in respect of money laundering?

A   Yes

B   No

The ICAEW Code of Ethics in respect of professional behaviour?

C   Yes

D   No   LO 3e

36 Harriet is the Money Laundering Reporting Officer of Maldon and Braintree, a firm of chartered accountants. A trainee in the firm suspects that an excessive amount of cash sales in a client's accounts signifies laundered funds, and reports this suspicion to Harriet. Harriet immediately notifies the National Crime Agency.

It is later discovered that the cash sales were genuine and that no money laundering has taken place.

Can the client take legal action against Maldon and Braintree for breach of confidentiality?

A   Yes

B   No

Is Harriet in breach of the ICAEW Code of Ethics in respect of confidentiality?

C   Yes

D   No   LO 3e

37 Which cybercrime threat is described below?

Criminals record what the user types onto their keyboard

A   Phishing

B   Keylogging

C   Ad clicker

D   Screenshot manager   LO 3g

38 Angelina was recently sent an email that appeared to be from her bank. It instructed her to click on a link and confirm some of her security information. Just days later she noticed that someone had transferred money out of her bank account.

Angelina has been the victim of phishing.

A   True

B   False

This is an example of fraud by abuse of position.

C   True

D   False   LO 3g

39 Which of the following would be offences under the Computer Misuse Act 1990?

(1)   The creation of ransomware

(2)   Accidentally spreading a computer virus

(3)   Hacking a private computer network

(4)   Accessing a colleague's email account by guessing their username and password

A   (1) and (4) only

B   (1), (3) and (4) only

C   All of the above

D   (3) and (4) only   LO 3f

Chapter 11: Employment, data protection and intellectual property law

1   Gary works for the owner of the local country hotel, Oasis Ltd, as a self-employed gardener. There is no question of Gary being an employee. Which of the following best describes the legal status of the arrangement between Gary and Oasis Ltd?

A   A contract of employment

B   A contract of service

C   A contract for services

D   A contract of agency   LO 4c

2   Which of the following factors is consistent with there being a contract of service between Fred and the company for which he works, Newbuild Ltd?

A   Fred is not allowed to delegate his work

B   Fred is paid gross

C   Fred is to purchase and maintain his own tools

D   Fred can wear what he likes to work   LO 4c

3   Ivy works at Gorgeous Flowers Ltd. Which of the following factors is consistent with her being treated as self-employed?

A   Ivy's employer deducts tax at source

B   Ivy wears a Gorgeous Flowers apron at work

C   Ivy is entitled to holiday pay

D   Ivy provides her own car for delivering flowers   LO 4c

4   Are the following statements true or false in relation to determining whether a working arrangement is between an employer and employee **or** between an employer and an independent contractor?

Provided there is an element of control and personal service and mutuality of obligations present, then the arrangement is a contract of employment.

A   True

B   False

Where a person is only offered work on an as-and-when required basis by their employer, the working arrangement cannot be a contract of service.

C   True

D   False   LO 4c

5   Larry works as a driver for Wally's Wine Warehouses. He wears a Wally's Wine uniform and drives a Wally's Wine van belonging to his employer. He is paid gross and accounts for tax and national insurance himself. Each day, he is told by the manager of Wally's Wine what to deliver and to whom. He is allowed to ask his wife to make deliveries for him in the event that he is ill. He is not permitted to work for anyone else and is entitled to receive six weeks' holiday pay from Wally's Wine. Which of the following best describes Larry's employment status?

   A   He is an independent contractor because he is paid gross and accounts for tax and national insurance himself

   B   He is an employee. The fact that he is paid gross is not conclusive and the other factors point to him being an employee

   C   He is an independent contractor because there is not a sufficient level of personal service for a contract of employment to exist, since his wife is allowed to do his work for him in the event that he is ill

   D   He is an employee because the fact that he is only permitted to delegate in limited circumstances means that he cannot be an independent contractor   LO 4c

---

6   Bun the Bakers Ltd has a number of retail outlets in London. Flora works for the company when it is short-staffed during particularly busy periods. She wears a Bun the Bakers apron and hat and is given 24 hours' notice of which outlet she is required to work at. She then has the use of the Bun the Baker van for any deliveries. She is not entitled to ask anyone else to perform her duties. Tax and national insurance is deducted from her pay at source. Work is offered to Flora by Bun the Bakers on an as-and-when required basis. Which of the following best describes her employment status?

   A   Flora is an employee, because tax is deducted from her pay at source

   B   Flora is an independent contractor because she is only given 24 hours' notice of when she is required to work

   C   Flora is an independent contractor because she is only offered work by Bun the Bakers on an as-and-when required basis

   D   Flora is an employee because the majority of factors considered in the multiple test point towards a contract of service   LO 4c

---

7   Do each of the following statements accurately state a legal consequence of someone being held to be an 'employee' rather than an independent contractor?

   They do not need to make national insurance contributions whereas an independent contractor does.

   A   Yes

   B   No

   They are able to bring a claim for wrongful dismissal.

   C   Yes

   D   No   LO 4c

8   Are the following legal consequences of someone being held to be an 'independent contractor' rather than an employee?

They may need to register for and charge VAT.

A   Yes

B   No

They have the right to bring a claim for unfair dismissal under the Employment Rights Act 1996.

C   Yes

D   No   LO 4c

9   Are the following legal consequences of someone being held to be an employee rather than an independent contractor?

The employer must deduct income tax from the salary paid to an employee.

A   Yes

B   No

The employee will be entitled to protection under health and safety legislation unlike an independent contractor.

C   Yes

D   No   LO 4c

10 Are the following statements true or false?

A contract of employment must be either in writing or evidenced in writing.

A   True

B   False

The law may imply terms into a contract of employment even where the parties to it have not expressly agreed that they should be included.

C   True

D   False   LO 4d

11 Within what time period must an employer provide a written statement of employment particulars to an employee following the commencement of their employment (in the absence of an employment contract)?

A   14 days

B   28 days

C   2 months

D   3 months   LO 4d

12   In the event that an employer fails to comply with the requirement under the Employment Rights Act 1996 to provide a written statement of employment particulars:

Does the employer face potential criminal liability, for example a fine or period of imprisonment?

A   Yes

B   No

Does the employer face potential civil liability in cases even where there is a written contract of employment covering the matters which should be contained within the written statement of employment particulars?

C   Yes

D   No   LO 4d

13   Marmaduke is employed by Fashions First Ltd to order the new season's clothing for men from various suppliers. In many cases, when he places an order, he receives a commission from the supplier and keeps this commission for himself, regarding it as a perk of the job. In respect of which implied common law duty is Marmaduke in breach?

A   The duty of fidelity

B   The duty to obey lawful and reasonable orders

C   The duty not to misuse confidential information

D   The duty to exercise reasonable care and skill   LO 4d

14   Are the following statements true or false?

An employee owes a duty under the common law to obey their employer's instructions at all times.

A   True

B   False

An employee's implied duties under the common law cease when their employment ceases.

C   True

D   False   LO 4d

15   Are the following implied duties of the employer in a contract of employment?

To assess the employee's performance on an annual basis.

A   Yes

B   No

To pay reasonable remuneration.

C   Yes

D   No   LO 4d

16 Amran is employed on a part-time basis by Lord Noble, to manage his portfolio of property and equities. He is paid on a commission only basis. The parties have agreed that Amran will be paid an agreed commission every time he makes a profit on a sale transaction for Lord Noble. Last year, Amran was very happy with his earnings but in the past eight months, he has earned very little because Lord Noble has been planning a new business project and has failed to give Amram instructions when requested.

Might Lord Noble be liable for breach of his common law duty to pay Amran remuneration?

A Yes

B No

Might Lord Noble be liable for breach of his common law duty to provide Amran with work?

C Yes

D No   LO 4d

17 Are the following statements true or false?

An employer has a common law duty not to pass confidential information to a third party about an employee.

A True

B False

An employer owes a common law duty to provide an accurate and fair reference for their employee on termination of their employment.

C True

D False   LO 4d

18 Arthur works at a timber yard owned and operated by Tall Trees plc. One day he is stacking timber ready for shipment and one of the saws, being operated nearby, becomes detached from its station and causes Arthur serious injury. It transpires that Conrad, the director responsible for health and safety issues at Tall Trees plc, has failed to have its machinery serviced for more than three years. Tall Trees plc has also been criticised for failing to separate its stacking yard from the operational sawing works. Which of the following best describes the legal position?

A Tall Trees plc and Conrad are liable to a fine up to £50,000

B Tall Trees plc is liable to an unlimited fine

C Tall Trees plc is liable to an unlimited fine and Conrad is liable to up to two years' imprisonment

D Conrad is liable to a fine and imprisonment for up to two years and Tall Trees plc is liable to an unlimited fine   LO 4d

19 Abigail has been working for Comfy Sofas Ltd for 18 months but her employment contract does not specify a notice period in the event of termination. What is the minimum period of notice to which she is entitled under the Employment Rights Act 1996?

    A   At least five days

    B   At least a week

    C   At least two weeks

    D   At least one month   LO 4d

20 Zak has recently been given one month's notice by Firezone Ltd to terminate his employment. He has been working for Firezone Ltd for five years and asks you whether his notice period is sufficient. Which of the following best sums up the advice you should give him?

    A   Yes. His contract provides for the giving of one month's notice

    B   Yes. The common law requires his employer to give him a reasonable period of notice and one month is reasonable

    C   Yes. Under the Employment Rights Act 1996 he is entitled to a minimum period of one month's notice

    D   No. Under the Employment Rights Act 1996 he is entitled to a minimum period of five weeks' notice   LO 4d

21 Martha has been working for Mark-Up Cars Ltd for 13 years. What is the statutory minimum notice period to which she is entitled under the Employment Rights Act 1996?

    A   At least one month

    B   At least 13 weeks

    C   At least 12 weeks

    D   At least one year   LO 4d

22 Under the Acas Code of Practice on disciplinary and grievance issues, is an employee to be given the right to appeal when a decision is made against them?

    A   Yes

    B   No

    Does a breach of the Acas Code of Practice render an associated dismissal automatically unfair?

    C   Yes

    D   No   LO 4d

23 Are the following statements true or false?

An employee has a statutory right not to be unfairly dismissed under the Employment Rights Act 1996.

A   True

B   False

An employee who does not comply with the Acas Code of Practice may have their claim reduced by up to 50%.

C   True

D   False   LO 4d

24 In most claims for unfair dismissal, the employee must have been continuously employed for a prescribed period with the same or an associated employer. However, there are some types of dismissal which are regarded as automatically unfair under statute and consequently no period of continuous service has to be accrued by the employee concerned. Which of the following reasons for dismissal is regarded as automatically unfair?

A   Where an employee is dismissed because they have committed a serious assault on a fellow employee

B   Where an employee, who works as a chauffeur, has been dismissed because they have had their licence revoked for drink-driving offences

C   Where an employee has been dismissed without the statutory disciplinary and dismissal procedure in the Employment Act 2002 being followed

D   Where an employee has been dismissed on the grounds of redundancy   LO 4e

25 Within what period of time following the effective date of termination of an employee's employment contract must an employee make a claim for unfair dismissal?

A   28 days

B   One month

C   Three months

D   Six months   LO 4e

26 Nathan is employed by Clifford to manage the catering at a conference of the South East Police Service in Brighton over a two-week period. Which of the following would not constitute dismissal for the purposes of an unfair dismissal claim?

A   If Clifford were to tell him a month in advance that he has found someone to provide the same services more cheaply and Nathan is not required

B   If Clifford were to send Nathan home on the third day because the vol-au-vents were uncooked

C   If Clifford were to say that he was no longer needed Nathan because fewer delegates than expected had attended the conference

D   If the conference were to be cancelled because a large proportion of the delegates were required to report for duty in view of a major earthquake in Brighton   LO 4e

27 Are the following statements true or false?

An employee is not required to show a qualifying period of continuous employment if the principal reason for their dismissal is that they have made a protected disclosure.

A   True

B   False

Dismissal on the grounds of an employee's membership or non-membership of a trade union or due to the fact that they are involved in trade union activities is automatically unfair.

C   True

D   False   LO 4e

28 In the absence of an automatically unfair reason for dismissal, must an employer's decision to dismiss an employee satisfy the following conditions?

The employer must show that their principal reason for dismissing the employee is one of the potentially fair reasons contained in the Employment Rights Act 1996.

A   Yes

B   No

The employer must have acted reasonably in the circumstances.

C   Yes

D   No   LO 4e

29 Sophia has worked as a nurse in the Sunshine Care Home for two years. She was injured in a traffic accident while taking some of its residents on a day trip in the home's minibus, driven by one of her colleagues, Raphael. Although she returned to work soon after the accident, it left her with neck and back pains that were aggravated by her work, which involved lifting and bathing residents. Her employer allowed her time off work to keep doctor and hospital appointments and warned her that if she failed to improve, she would have to leave or accept a change of position to work on reception instead. Sophia failed to get better but really did not wish to be a receptionist. Two weeks later, she was informed in writing that her employment with Sunshine Care Home would be terminated as a result of her decision not to take up the receptionist post. Which of the following best describes Sophia's dismissal?

A   Automatically unfair because Sophia's absenteeism was due to an injury caused by someone employed by the Sunshine Care Home

B   Potentially fair but the Sunshine Care Home, by taking the decision to dismiss Sophia, has acted unreasonably in the circumstances

C   Potentially unfair because the receptionist job does not constitute suitable alternative employment for Sophia

D   Potentially fair and the Sunshine Care Home has acted reasonably in the circumstances by giving Sophia time off work and an offer of an alternative job. Her employer cannot be expected to keep her job open indefinitely   LO 4e

30 Greta, aged 61, had worked for Fine Fabrics for 25 years and the employment tribunal has ruled that she was unfairly dismissed. Which of the following may be relevant to the calculation of the basic award to which she will be entitled?

   (1) Greta's age

   (2) Greta's length of service

   (3) Greta's conduct

   (4) Any redundancy payment made to Greta

   A   (1) and (2) only

   B   (2) and (3) only

   C   (2), (3) and (4) only

   D   All of the above   LO 4e

31 Under the Employment Rights Act 1996 can a compensatory award for unfair dismissal be reduced in the following circumstances?

Where the employee's conduct causes or contributes to their dismissal.

   A   Yes

   B   No

Where the employee fails to mitigate their loss, eg, by seeking employment elsewhere.

   C   Yes

   D   No   LO 4e

32 What is the usual remedy awarded for wrongful dismissal?

   A   Compensatory award

   B   Reinstatement

   C   Damages

   D   Injunction   LO 4e

33 Oliver has been employed by Hots Ltd to deliver pizza for the past 10 months. His manager, Charles, regularly turns up for work drunk and swears at Oliver and one day accuses him of having made a pass at his girlfriend, which is not true. Charles then pushes Oliver off his delivery bike and tells him to get lost. Oliver leaves and has not been back to work at Hots Ltd since.

Can Oliver bring a claim for unfair constructive dismissal?

   A   Yes

   B   No

Can Oliver bring an action for wrongful dismissal?

   C   Yes

   D   No   LO 4e

34 Raita works as a receptionist for Bayview Hotel. Her contract provides that the employer may terminate the contract without notice but subject to paying the equivalent of six months' salary. After working there for only nine months, Raita is handed notice of termination with immediate effect. Which of the following best describes her legal position?

   A   Raita can bring an action for wrongful dismissal without notice

   B   Raita is unable to bring an action because she has only been employed for nine months

   C   Raita has no right to sue for wrongful dismissal but may enforce the obligation to pay six months' salary

   D   Raita may bring an action for wrongful dismissal and damages will be the equivalent of six months' salary
                                                                                                    LO 4e

35 Arthur works as an accountant for the Churchill High School. He embezzles £30,000 of the school's funds and is subsequently arrested and charged with theft. The Governors of the school dismiss him from his post with immediate effect following a disciplinary hearing, during the course of which Arthur was offered the right to appeal against their final decision but turned it down. Which of the following best describes the legal position?

   A   The school is justified in dismissing Arthur without notice, as he has engaged in gross misconduct and the school therefore has no liability, particularly since disciplinary and dismissal procedures appear to have been followed

   B   The school is justified in dismissing Arthur (as he has engaged in gross misconduct) and will only be liable for nominal damages as a result of terminating his contract with less than the statutory minimum period of notice under the Employment Rights Act 1996

   C   The school is liable for wrongful dismissal, as a reasonable employer would have given Arthur a warning first in the circumstances

   D   Arthur is entitled to claim wrongful dismissal because he has been dismissed in breach of his employment contract
                                                                                                    LO 4e

36 Are the following statements true or false?

   Redundancy is a form of dismissal.

   A   True

   B   False

   A statutory redundancy payment is calculated in the same way as the basic award in unfair dismissal cases.

   C   True

   D   False   LO 4f

37 Kevin has been working as a payroll clerk in the local office of Bespoke Windows Ltd for the past 18 months. When the company installs new IT systems for all its financial and administrative operations, it informs Kevin that he is no longer required and advertises for a new employee who is competent in the use of its new IT system (which Kevin is not).

Has Kevin been made redundant in accordance with the Employment Rights Act 1996?

A   Yes

B   No

Is Kevin entitled to claim a statutory redundancy payment under the Employment Rights Act 1996?

C   Yes

D   No   LO 4f

38 Hamish has been made redundant from his post as coach for the Highland Huskies football team. Within what time period, following the relevant date of his dismissal by reason of redundancy, must he bring a claim for a statutory redundancy payment in accordance with the Employment Rights Act 1996?

A   Three months

B   Six months

C   Twelve months

D   Two years   LO 4f

39 Jack works for Complete Gardens Ltd, servicing and renovating lawnmowers. As the company plans to concentrate on the sale of plants and garden furniture, it closes down its machinery section which is responsible for servicing and renovating lawnmowers. The company offers Jack a new post on the same premises, being in charge of removing dead or diseased plants, as directed by the company's horticultural expert. It also offers to pay him the same salary. He refuses.

Has Jack been made redundant in accordance with the Employment Rights Act 1996?

A   Yes

B   No

Is Jack entitled to claim a statutory redundancy payment under the Employment Rights Act 1996?

C   Yes

D   No   LO 4f

40 Legal and economic consequences that would follow a finding that a worker is employed under a contract of service would include the following:

Potentially they have the right to claim unfair dismissal.

A   Yes

B   No

They should be paid gross and account for income tax to HMRC themselves.

C   Yes

D   No   Sample Paper LO 4c

41 Andrew has undertaken work as a lorry driver for Hopeless Haulage Ltd for the past three years under the following terms:

He is responsible for maintaining his own lorry. He pays his own tax and national insurance and may substitute another lorry driver for himself, but only on receipt of written permission from the company.

Advise Andrew as to whether he is in fact an employee by indicating whether or not each of the following statements is true or false:

Andrew is under a degree of financial risk. This is inconsistent with a contract of employment.

A   True

B   False

The fact that Andrew's ability to delegate his work is limited is consistent with the existence of a contract of employment.

C   True

D   False   Sample Paper LO 4c

---

42 Sources of contractual terms which can come together to form an employment contract include the following:

Terms implied by the common law.

A   Yes

B   No

Terms contained in a written statement of employment particulars where the employee has signed the statement itself.

C   Yes

D   No   Sample Paper LO 4d

---

43 David is a journalist working for the Daily Libel at their Southampton office.

David has a clause in his contract which states that he can be required to work from any other office of the company on a temporary basis provided that the office is not more than 200 miles from the Southampton office. For the past two months, David who lives in Southampton has been required to work every day at the company's Nottingham office, some 170 miles away from Southampton. David has consistently argued with his employers that the daily travelling to Nottingham is destroying his health due to exhaustion and stress, and that he presents a serious health and safety risk to other road users and other employees of the Nottingham office.

Advise the Daily Libel of any potential claims David could make against them by indicating whether or not each of the following statements is true or false.

David could claim that they are in breach of their common law duty to protect him against reasonably foreseeable risks to his health, safety and welfare.

A   True

B   False

The outcome of a successful claim for breach of a common law duty by an employer is for an employee to be awarded damages.

C   True

D   False   Sample Paper LO 4d

44 Circumstances under which a wrongful dismissal can occur include where:

A fixed-term contract is terminated by the employer before the date it was due to expire.

A   Yes

B   No

The employer terminates the employment without notice, or with less notice than the employee is entitled to receive under the terms of their contract or the Employment Rights Act 1996.

C   Yes

D   No   Sample Paper LO 4e

45 The dismissal of an employee will constitute an automatically unfair dismissal if it is on the grounds of:

Trade union membership or activities.

A   Yes

B   No

Taking certain types of action on Health & Safety grounds, eg, raising a concern with a Health & Safety Representative.

C   Yes

D   No   LO 4e

46 When determining the fairness of a dismissal on the grounds of capability or qualifications:

It is sufficient that the employer honestly believes on reasonable grounds that an employee is incapable of carrying out the job that they are employed to do.

A   True

B   False

It is not necessary for there to be a contractual obligation (express or implied) to hold the relevant qualification in order to be dismissed fairly on the grounds of lack of 'qualifications'.

C   True

D   False   Sample Paper LO 4e

47 In relation to claims for a statutory redundancy payment under the Employment Rights Act 1996 are the following statements true or false?

An employee must have accrued one year's continuous service with the same or an associated employer at the relevant date in order to be able to claim.

A   True

B   False

An employee must have been dismissed, laid off or put on short-time working in order to be able to claim.

C   True

D   False   Sample Paper LO 4f

48 Are the following statements true or false?

The Data Protection Act 1998 applies to computer-based and electronically stored information systems only.

A   True

B   False

The Act aims to protect individuals from the use of incorrect information and the misuse of correct, but confidential, information.

C   True

D   False   LO 4a

49 With regard to the Data Protection Act 1998:

Can a data controller be either an individual or a company?

A   Yes

B   No

Are data subject to the Act's regulation, if they merely record the holder's opinion about the subject, rather than facts about them?

C   Yes

D   No   LO 4a

50 Homemade Cakes Ltd holds data about its employees. The company secretary, Snoop, seeks your advice as to whether there are any penalties in the event of non-compliance with the Data Protection Act 1998, as he is concerned that certain aspects of it may have been overlooked. He has been told that, if there is breach of the Act, there may be:

(1) civil liability

(2) criminal liability

(3) a court order directing the forfeiture, destruction or erasing of databases.

Advise Snoop on the issue of liability:

A   There is potential liability for all of (1), (2) and (3)

B   There is potential liability to (2) only

C   There is potential liability to (2) and (3) only

D   There is potential liability to none of the above   LO 4a

51 The managing director of Garden Gnomes Ltd asks you whether the company is required to register in any way in relation to the Data Protection Act 1998. You advise him that the company has an obligation to notify the Information Commissioner, who maintains a register showing the types of data, the purpose for which it is held and who the data subjects are. He then wants to know whether the following are true or false.

Failure to notify the Information Commissioner is a criminal offence.

A   True

B   False

The Information Commissioner's register relates to all data controllers in the UK but is not accessible to the public.

C   True

D   False   LO 4a

52 With regard to the eight data protection principles under the Data Protection Act 1998, are the following statements true or false?

The data controller is obliged to ensure that personal data shall not be transferred outside the European Economic Area, unless the country or territory to which it is transferred ensures an adequate level of protection for data subjects.

A   True

B   False

The data controller must keep the data subject informed (and supply copies) of all personal data held or processed in respect of that data subject.

C   True

D   False   LO 4a

53 With regard to the rights given to data subjects by the Data Protection Act 1998, answer the following.

Is the data subject always entitled to compensation in the event that the data controller is found to have inaccurate data?

A   Yes

B   No

Does the data subject have the right to take action to destroy any inaccurate data held about them?

C   Yes

D   No   LO 4a

54 Amy is treasurer to the Copse Golf Club, an unincorporated association. Amy is invited to apply for the position of treasurer to the Forest Green Golf Club. Amy duly applies and the President of the Copse Golf Club passes on all the information which it holds about Amy to the Forest Green Golf Club. However, Amy is not offered the position with the Forest Green Golf Club and has become convinced that it is because of information received from the Copse Golf Club. She has consulted the Copse Golf Club rules and there is nothing there that gives her the right to see her records. She wants to know if she is entitled to have access to them under the Data Protection Act 1998.

Is she entitled to have access to her records at the Copse Golf Club, under the Act?

A   Yes

B   No

If she can show that the new post was not offered to her because of the information that was supplied, whether or not it was accurate, is she entitled to compensation under the Data Protection Act?

C   Yes

D   No   LO 4a

55 The Data Protection Act 1998 provides certain rights for data subjects. Are the following true or false in relation to the rights of data subjects set out in the Act?

A data subject has a right to access data held about them unless the data are held in encoded form when access requires a court order.

A   True

B   False

A data subject whose rights have been infringed, in that inaccurate data about them have been held, can take action to rectify the inaccurate data but cannot obtain compensation if they have suffered damage by reason of the inaccurate data.

C   True

D   False   Sample Paper LO 4a

56 Linehouse are an up-and-coming band that enjoys writing and recording its own music. The band members are concerned that any music that they create and distribute online could be at risk from others copying and selling it as their own music.

Is copyright the most appropriate method of the band protecting their music?

A   Yes

B   No

Does copyright have to be applied for?

C   Yes

D   No   LO 4b

57 Loren is a sole trader who recently designed a new product that she created a distinctive name and logo for. Which of the following methods of protection could Loren use to protect the product's name and logo?

A   Patent

B   Registered design

C   Design right

D   Trademark   LO 4b

58 Alltech Ltd has made an improvement to the design of the vacuum cleaners it produces. The improvement involves a small electronic part that fits into an otherwise standard vacuum cleaner to increase performance. The company would like to protect the design of the new electronic part. Which of the following methods of protection should Alltech Ltd use?

A   Registered design

B   Copyright

C   Patent

D   Design right   LO 4b

Answer Bank

   Law: Answer Bank

1   C   Such an agreement must be in writing (the transfer itself must be by deed).

2   B   False. Legislation often implies terms to protect the weaker party, notwithstanding any express provision in the contract (for example the supply of Goods and Services Act 1982).

      D   False. An adult not of sound mind, for example, does not have capacity.

3   B   Voidable. For example where a party enters a contract as a result of undue influence, they may elect to avoid the contract.

4   C   Unenforceable. A contract for the sale of land must be in writing.

5   C   The written evidence must be signed or acknowledged in some way by Gary.

6   D   Acceptance will only be effective to create the agreement (that is an essential element of a contract), if the accepting party is aware of the offer.

7   B   No. The flyer from Clarence is merely an invitation to treat.

      D   No. He cannot be in breach of contract since no contract has been made. He is simply rejecting Kenton's offer (which is made in response to Clarence's invitation to treat).

8   B   No. The display constitutes an invitation to treat only.

      C   Yes. An offer is made by Matilda when she takes the roses to the till and proffers £6. The shopkeeper is free to accept or reject that offer.

9   C   Advertisements are generally invitations to treat.

10   C   When a pre-condition is satisfied, the offer becomes unconditional.

11   A   If the event or circumstances on which an offer is conditional does or do not transpire, the offer is no longer capable of acceptance and is terminated.

12   B   No, Hilda's reply on Tuesday constitutes a counter offer which terminates George's offer.

13   D   The offer remains capable of acceptance (at least for a reasonable time). Mary is simply asking for information about when she can make payment.

14   B   Nathan's reply is a counter offer which Mark accepts. He should have revoked his counter offer on buying the tandem from eBay by communicating that fact to Mark.

15   B   False. The offeror may still revoke the offer within that three-month period, unless they have bound themselves to keep it open by a separate contract.

      D   False. The postal rule applies to acceptance only and not to revocation.

16   D   There must be some act on the part of the offeree to indicate their acceptance.

17   B   No. The 'postal rule' does not apply to revocation.

      D   No. The acceptance takes effect when it is posted on 1 June (assuming postal acceptance was within the contemplation of the parties) with the result that there is a binding contract at that point.

18   A   True.

      D   False. The offeror may waive the requirement for acceptance to be communicated (either expressly or by implication).

19   B   Yes. Peter's revocation is not effective until received by Quentin.

20   B   False. The law has not yet provided a clear statement of when an acceptance sent by email becomes effective.

      C   True.

21 A   True. The offeror would need to be very specific indeed for this not to be the case.

    D   False. The offeree may use any reasonable method.

22 B   No. When acceptance is to be made 'by notice in writing', this means that notice is required to be received by the offeror and the postal rule does not apply.

    D   No, because there is no valid acceptance.

23 A   Carol's acceptance is effective when posted. A revocation is ineffective until received (which, in this case, is after the contract becomes binding on the posting of the acceptance on 5th January).

24 A   Yes, if it can be shown that the document was not intended to comprise all the agreed terms (otherwise the general rule applies, that oral evidence cannot be admitted to add to, vary or contradict written terms).

    C   Yes. The express term will prevail.

25 C   The fact that the arrangement concerns property does not mean that the presumption does not apply, but is evidence of its rebuttal.

26 A   True.

    D   False. The presumption is rebuttable.

27 C   Consideration must have some identifiable value ('sufficient') but does not need to be equal in value to the consideration received in return ('adequate').

28 A   Yes. Such a rent may not be adequate but it is sufficient which makes it valid consideration.

    C   Yes. This is valid consideration.

29 C   Performance of an existing contractual duty owed to the promisor is not valid consideration.

30 A   The value of the bicycle is irrelevant. It is something to which Eve was not previously entitled.

31 B   There is no consideration for the waiver of the additional £20 to which Oscar is entitled. The lesser sum in D is sufficient because it is to be paid early.

32 A   True.

    C   True (provided that such implied terms are not inconsistent with express terms in the contract).

33 D   Phillip has given no consideration and is not a party to the contract. He has no rights to enforce the contract.

34 C   The third party must be identified. Either the contract must expressly provide that the third party can enforce it or the term must confer a benefit on them (unless it appears that the contracting parties did not intend them to be able to enforce the right). The Act allows enforcement of exclusion clauses as well as positive rights.

35 B   False. On the contrary, there is a rebuttable presumption that parties to a social or domestic agreement do not intend to create legal relations.

    C   True. However, this presumption is rebuttable.   SAMPLE PAPER

36 A   True. As a general rule, an advertisement in a newspaper is an invitation to treat which, unlike an offer, cannot be accepted to form a legally binding contract.   SAMPLE PAPER

    C   True. No contract is formed without agreement between the parties (usually in the form of an offer and an acceptance).   SAMPLE PAPER

37 D   Louise's performance of the works for which Matt promises a laptop, is past consideration and not valid. However, the contract between Matt and Adam is binding as there is a promise to pay for services promised in return.   SAMPLE PAPER

38 A   The postal rule applies, which means that Beth's acceptance is effective on posting. The postal rule does not apply to revocation, which must be communicated to the offeree. The purported revocation is ineffective, therefore, as it does not occur before acceptance on 3 February.   SAMPLE PAPER

39 A   Yes. Rejection of an offer terminates it. It cannot subsequently be accepted.

    C   Yes. An offer is deemed to lapse after a reasonable period of time (in the absence of an express provision or a separate option contract).   SAMPLE PAPER

40 D   It is probably unrealistic to imagine that major works would have been undertaken with no contract being in place. However, the terms of that contract will be a question of fact in all the circumstances and cannot readily be assumed.

Law: Answer Bank

1   C   It may also be known as a divisible contract.

2   C   Substantial performance is a sufficient discharge of a party's contractual obligations but entitles the other party to seek redress in respect of the part not completed.

3   C   The Act aims to reflect the fact that neither party is to blame for the contract coming to an end.

4   A   True.

      C   True. The amount ordered to be paid will be such amount as the court considers just, having regard to all the circumstances of the case.

5   A   True.

      D   False. He may treat the contract as discharged and sue for damages.

6   C   Damage not arising in the ordinary course of things is only recoverable to the extent that it is in the reasonable contemplation of the parties at the time of making the contract as the probable result of the breach.

7   B   False. Damages are intended to put the party in the position they would have been in had the contract been performed.

      D   False. The claimant is required to take only reasonable steps, not ones that carry undue risk or that are discreditable.

8   D   The sum of £5,000 is likely to be regarded as penal in nature and not in proportion to the legitimate interest of the innocent party. As such it is likely to be a penalty clause and necessarily void. Had the sum been smaller (say £50) it would have been in proportion to the interest of the innocent party (the prevention of errors or delays in advertising) and it would have been a valid liquidated damages clause.

9   B   James is in breach of contract and therefore liable to pay damages, but Jeremy is unlikely to be able to show any outstanding loss.

10   B   The amount of £150 when compared against the contract price is only 1.5% per day and would not be thought of as excessive. It is intended to protect Siegfried's legitimate interest of ensuring the work is completed on schedule and is therefore a valid liquidated damages clause.

11   B   Specific performance is unlikely to be ordered in such a case because of the difficulties in supervising compliance with the award.

12   D   Because it is a negative promise (ie, an agreement not to do something) that requires to be enforced. A mandatory injunction compels positive action and specific performance is unsuitable because it should require supervision. A quantum meruit award or claim is relevant where one party has been prevented from completing their performance of a contract but deserves to be paid for partial performance.

13   B   No. Clauses that exclude liability for negligence are only void if unreasonable.

      D   No. A contract between two private individuals is not subject to UCTA.

14   B   This is how the test is expressed in the Act. The parties' relative bargaining strengths (D) will be taken into account, as well as whether any inducement was offered and whether the innocent party knew, or should have known of the term.

15   A   Damages for losses sustained are recoverable to the extent that they are reasonably foreseeable and not too remote. The losses claimed under the first head can be described as arising in the ordinary course of business and are likely to be recoverable. However, those under the second head are too remote. Even if Foul Foods Ltd had been able to bid for the lucrative contract, there is no certainty that the company would have been awarded the contract.   SAMPLE PAPER

16   B   False. Specific performance is not usually awarded in cases of personal service.

       D   False. Likewise specific performance is unlikely in such a contract, where supervision would be required.   SAMPLE PAPER

17   D   There is nothing to prevent the parties from continuing to settle the dispute themselves and the courts will actively encourage alternative forms of dispute resolution.

Chapter 3: Agency

1   C   The agent effectively drops out of the picture. The third party can also be sued on the contract.

2   A   True.

    D   False. It can be oral unless the agent is to execute a deed, in which case the appointment must be by deed. It is usual to appoint an agent in writing in commercial transactions.

3   A   Yes. An agency by estoppel has arisen, by virtue of the supplier relying on the continuing representation by Lady Grey that Arthur is her agent.

    C   Yes. She is estopped from denying the agency relationship. However, she may seek to reclaim the money from Arthur.

4   D   Although Stephen acted in good faith and possibly reasonably (and was clearly unable to contact Anthony), the law is unlikely to say that an agency of necessity has arisen, because it is not inclined to allow a person to be bound by the act of a complete stranger.

5   B   No. It is the conduct of the principal that might give rise to an agency by estoppel, not the conduct of the 'agent'.

    D   No. The contract can only be enforced against Scarlett personally.

6   B   No. A principal cannot ratify a part of a contract only.

    C   Yes.

7   A   Yes. Ratification needs more than passive inactivity but can be inferred from words or conduct.

    D   No, because the contract has been ratified.

8   B   False. Ratification has retrospective effect as if the principal were the original contracting party and the agent no longer has any liability on the contract. The third party must, therefore, sue the principal.

    C   True.

9   B   An agent has a duty to account for all monies received as a result of being an agent.

10 B   No. Generally speaking, an agent owes a duty to provide personal performance and not to delegate it to another person.

    D   No. An agent must respect the duty of confidentiality even after the agency relationship has ended.

11 A   True.

    C   True.

12 B   No. In the absence of express provision, a reasonable amount of remuneration is payable.

    C   Yes. An agent has the right to exercise a lien over property of the principal pending payment of sums owed.

13 A   A partner has implied usual authority to do usual things that a partner might do. The purchase of office supplies is likely to be considered a usual activity for most partnerships.

14 C   Ostensible authority can arise through acquiescence of the other partners. It can also be wider than implied authority (which must be usual or incidental).

15 C   An agency by estoppel has arisen because Kelvin and Oscar were content to allow Barry to act as managing director and Barry has ostensible or apparent authority to bind the company.

16 A   True.

    D   False. There must be a causal link between the third party's loss and their reliance upon the representation.

17 B   False. There is no such requirement.

    C   True. Otherwise, the principal may find themselves still liable if the agent enters into further contracts with the third party without authority and the third party is unaware that they are no longer an agent.

18 A   By calling her his 'buying partner', Vincent has given the impression that Roz was his agent and that she had the authority to purchase goods on behalf of the company.

19 A   Yes. If it appears that the parties intended this to be the case, she may be liable.

    D   No. It means that it is more likely that she will be personally liable but, again, it is subject to the intentions of the parties.

20 A   Yes. In fact, either the agent or the principal can sue on the contract, but the agent's rights are subordinated to the principal's rights.

    C   Yes. Vince may sue either Ashley or Phyllis on the contract (but not both).

21 A   Yes.

    C   Yes. However, Barney can only enforce the contract against one or the other.

22 B   No. Not in the absence of ratification by her.

    C   Yes.

23 A   Yes. A principal appoints an agent to carry out a specific task or tasks.

    C   Yes. A principal can subsequently ratify a contract entered into between their agent and third party, subject to certain conditions being satisfied.   SAMPLE PAPER

24 A   Dennis is no longer a partner and there is no express or implied agency and no question of ratification. No agency arises on the basis of Dennis holding himself out to be a partner.
                                                                                                 SAMPLE PAPER

25 A   Yes. Express authority can be given orally or in writing.

    C   Yes. An agency by estoppel arises on the basis of a principal's conduct in holding out another person to be their agent.   SAMPLE PAPER

Chapter 4: Negligence

1　B　False. Damages are normally calculated to put the claimant in the position they would have been in, had the contract been performed.

　　C　True.

2　B　No. There may be damage to property for example.

　　C　Yes.

3　B　No. There does not need to be any relationship at all. Indeed the parties to a tort case are often complete strangers.

　　C　Yes. The question of public policy is one of several tests applied, but if public policy dictates that no duty should exist, then none shall exist.

4　B　This may be relevant when assessing damages but is not relevant to whether a duty of care exists at all.

5　A　*Res ipsa loquitur* is an argument by the claimant that 'the facts speak for themselves' in pointing to a breach on the part of the defendant. The burden of proof then shifts to the defendant to show that they were not negligent.

6　B　The defendant's lack of qualification will not be taken into account to reduce the relevant standard of care, which is that of a reasonable (qualified) driver. The fact that the claimant is especially vulnerable is only relevant to the standard of care applied, if the defendant is aware of that fact, and such knowledge has the effect of raising the standard of care to be met in discharging the duty of care.

7　B　No. The test will depend on knowledge and practice at the time of the incident.

　　D　No. The standard applied will be that of a reasonable man with the skill of a yard owner holding all the qualifications that Natasha holds.

8　A　True.

　　D　False. This is unlikely to be sufficient. He must provide evidence of a body of professional opinion which the court considers to be reasonable.

9　C　This is a difficult area of the law. However, it is likely that the conclusion would be that the tools carelessly left on the pavement caused the accident. The local authority may argue that Naomi was contributorily negligent in not taking sufficient care herself. The injury is likely to be considered to be too remote to give rise to any liability on John's part.

10　C　Contractual liability may arise where he gives the advice in performance of a contract. Tortious liability may arise even where there is no contractual or fiduciary relationship between the parties.

11　D　The facts are similar to the *Caparo* case. The basic view is that the accounts are intended to enable shareholders to exercise their rights regarding the management of the company and not to make investment decisions. (Special circumstances may apply, of course, so that a different conclusion is reached, but there are none in this case.)

12　C　The facts are similar to the *Caparo* case. There is no duty of care owed to potential lenders.

13　A　It was not known that George was planning to take control of the company.

14　B　There can be no liability for advice given on social or informal occasions unless there are exceptional circumstances (and there are not in this case).

15　A　Yes.

　　D　No. They will not have suffered any loss.

16　B　False. An offence is committed but it is punishable by a fine only.

　　D　False. Such an agreement may be valid.

17	B	No. Such a provision is void under s 532 Companies Act 2006 (but may be valid if contained in a liability limitation agreement that satisfies the provisions of that Act).
	C	Yes, provided such an agreement is contained in a valid liability limitation agreement or is restricted to an indemnity in respect of the costs of successfully defending any proceedings.
18	B	The court has already established the amount of loss and the proportion by which damages should be reduced to reflect Esther's contributory negligence.
19	A	Knowledge of risk is not sufficient, nor even consent to risk. However, the circumstances here are so extreme that she can be taken to have waived the duty of care owed to her by Neil and *volenti* is likely to be successful.
20	B	False. While you cannot exclude liability for personal injury, you may be able to exclude liability for other injury or damage, if reasonable to do so.
	D	False. The Unfair Contract Terms Act 1977 applies to business-to-business liability as well as to business-to-consumer liability.
21	B	No.
	D	No. What must be reasonably foreseeable is the **type of damage** suffered. Provided the type of damage suffered was reasonably foreseeable, it does not matter that it came about in an unexpected way nor that it was more or less extensive than was reasonably foreseeable.
22	A	True.
	D	False. Vicarious liability does not depend on the fault or endeavours of the employer.
23	A	Yes.
	D	No. Although the incident happened during a business audit, the act was not closely connected with his employment.
24	A	Yes. The fact that he is acting in breach of a prohibition against doing his job in a particular way, does not take the act outside the scope of his employment.
	C	Yes.
25	B	No. Lack of qualification or disability is not generally relevant. The standard applied will be that of a reasonable (qualified) accountant.
	C	Yes. In this case, the necessary causal link between Alice's negligent advice and Bashir's loss cannot be established. SAMPLE PAPER
26	C	Tariq could sue Susan in contract or tort for her negligent advice. He could also sue Calculator LLP which would be vicariously liable for the negligent advice of Susan in tort. SAMPLE PAPER
27	B	There is no duty of care owed to Rustom by any of these parties since the relevant tests are not satisfied (for example the need for a sufficient degree of proximity or special relationship). Laylem LLP owes no duty of care to existing shareholders considering their investments. SAMPLE PAPER
28	B	Vicarious liability only arises for an employee's tortious acts where those acts are committed in the course of their employment or they are sufficiently connected to their employment. Vicarious liability is not designed to punish the employer, rather to protect the victim of the tort. SAMPLE PAPER
29	D	There is no duty of care owed to Priya by Zebra & Co. Auditors do not generally owe a duty to potential investors in a company. SAMPLE PAPER
30	B	False. This will depend on the facts and the relationship between the parties.
	C	True. Generally speaking, sophisticated investors are likely to be considered responsible for their own actions.

1   B   No. The liability of the members may be limited, but the liability of the company is always unlimited.

     D   No. If a shareholder (A) bought their shares from another shareholder (B), A's liability is only in respect of the shares' nominal value. The unpaid amount of any premium is a debt owed by B. It does not pass to A with the shares.

2   D   Following *Macaura v Northern Assurance Co Ltd 1925*, the company (as a separate legal entity) has the insurable interest and should insure its own assets.

3   B   No. In the absence of fraud or an agency relationship based on the business activities of the companies, the separate legal personality of each company within a group will be recognised.

     C   Yes. In such circumstances, the veil will be lifted in order to identify the company as a Neverland company.

4   A   True. Similarly, where directors are also members, provisions such as those in respect of fraudulent trading and wrongful trading lift the veil between the company and its members to impose a liability for the company's wrongful acts.

     C   True.

5   B   No. A public company must be a limited company.

     D   No. The company should not commence trading until a trading certificate has been obtained.

6   A   Yes. A public limited company must have a company secretary.

     D   No. The share capital of a public limited company is subject to a statutory minimum, but that is currently £50,000.

7   C   A private limited company must have at least one director, a public limited company must have at least two directors.

8   B   Six months.

9   C   A, B and D are true of private limited companies only. A public limited company cannot exclude pre-emption rights, it must get a court order to reduce its capital and it cannot redeem shares out of its own capital.

10   B   False. In the event that none is provided, model articles prescribed by the Secretary of State will apply.

     C   True.

11   B   No. Not unless Paddy and the vendor gave rights to New Style Ltd under the Contracts (Rights of Third Parties) Act 1999.

     D   No, because it did not exist at the time the contract was made.

12   B   No. Simple Solutions Ltd is not bound because it is not a party to the contract.

     C   Yes. The contract takes effect as if it was entered into between the seller and Quentin personally.

13   A   Yes, by special resolution or otherwise as provided by its articles of association.

     D   No. The Secretary of State (or company names adjudicator) may order a change of name in certain circumstances.

14   A   Yes, on the basis that the articles can be implied into her contract of employment.

     D   No because her claim is not made in her capacity as member (but rather as company secretary) and the articles bind the company and its **members** as if each **member** had contracted to observe its provisions.

15   B   False. Alteration requires a special resolution (in accordance with the Companies Act 2006) but unanimous agreement or a court order is required to alter a provision for entrenchment.

    D   False. Nor can it provide that a provision for entrenchment cannot be amended.

16   A   Yes, but not to deprive Simon, the company's solicitor, of any right to accrued pay before the passing of the resolution.

    D   No. A member is not bound by an alteration made after their becoming a member, that requires them to purchase more shares or to increase their liability in any way.

17   A   Yes. However, they must not be made available for public inspection.

    D   No. It is not compulsory, but if the company does keep such a register, it must comply with the legislative provisions as to its availability for inspection.

18   B   No. Only quoted companies need do so.

    C   Yes (a public limited company must do so within six months).

19   B   No. It is not a small company as it satisfies the criteria as to employees (under 50) but not turnover (up to £10.2m) and balance sheet (up to £5.1m).

    C   Yes. A small company would be exempt (although 10% of its members could still require an audit) but this company does not qualify for such an exemption.

20   D   Borrowing is not within the implied usual authority of a company secretary, nor did he have express or ostensible authority.

21   B   A pre-incorporation contract is not enforceable by or against the company (that is not incorporated at the time).   SAMPLE PAPER

22   A   Yes. A memorandum of association needs to be submitted on application for incorporation of a company.

    D   No. A trading certificate is only required for a public company, not a private company.
                                                  SAMPLE PAPER

23   A   True. A company secretary normally has the authority to deal with all administrative matters. The exact scope of their authority will usually depend on the size and nature of the company.

    D   False. A company secretary does not normally have authority to deal with the purchase of property or borrowing.   SAMPLE PAPER

24   A   S 386 specifies that all companies must include (1) and (3). But since Cabbit Ltd deals in goods its accounts must also contain a statement of stock.   SAMPLE PAPER

25   C   As with all private companies, Whimsome Ltd must file its accounts within 9 months of its year-end.

26   B   False. Micro-entities must file a simplified profit and loss account and balance sheet.

    D   False. There are two compulsory notes for micro-entities which must be included in the accounts if relevant (advances to directors and financial commitments).

27   D   All insurance and banking companies must appoint an auditor. Only micro and small companies are exempt from audit, medium companies must appoint an auditor. Quoted companies must appoint an auditor. Not-for-profit companies that are subject to public sector audit are exempt from appointing an auditor.

Chapter 6: Companies: ownership and management

1   D   A de facto director is not formally appointed but, like a shadow director, is a director by virtue of their conduct. An alternate director is appointed by a director.

2   A   True.

     D   False. The director's actions remain valid notwithstanding a defective or void appointment.

3   A   True. A sole director can be a company secretary but not a company auditor.

     D   False. Under s 157 of the Companies Act 2006 a person may not be appointed a director of a company unless they are at least 16 years old.

4   A   Yes. A director can be removed on the passing of an ordinary resolution (with special notice).

     D   No. He may be entitled to sue for breach of contract as a result.

5   A   The facts are similar to those in *Bushell v Faith* where the House of Lords held that since shares may be issued with such rights as the company determines, there was nothing to stop a company giving weighted voting rights in this manner.

6   B   False. The Companies Act 2006 changed the previous law to provide that companies have unrestricted objects unless specifically restricted by the articles.

     D   False. Directors are not agents of the members and, therefore, are not subject to their instruction as to how to act.

7   C   Frank's authority arises from the conduct of Flora and Gale in allowing him to act as a managing director and is therefore ostensible or apparent authority.

8   C   The contract is within the implied usual authority of a managing director.

9   B   False. All the directors' duties in the Companies Act 2006 are stated to apply to shadow directors also.

     C   True.

10   D   The facts are similar to those in *Howard Smith Ltd v Ampol Petroleum Ltd*, in which an allotment for such a purpose was held to be unconstitutional and invalid.

11   B   False. A director is not in breach of this duty where they act in accordance with the company's constitution or with an agreement, entered into after due consideration, that restricts the future exercise of a director's discretion.

     C   True.

12   A   Yes.

     D   No. In a public company, the constitution must expressly allow such authorisation.

13   A   Yes. Usually the standard is that of a reasonably diligent person with the general knowledge, skill and experience that may reasonably be expected of someone performing their functions as director. However, the actual experience, knowledge and skill is also taken into account and may result in a higher standard being applied.

     C   Yes. Simply attending board meetings is not likely to be sufficient in the light of his business experience.

14   B   No. Disclosure is sufficient unless the constitution provides otherwise.

     D   No. Disclosure to the board is sufficient unless the constitution provides otherwise.

15   B   False. In certain circumstances, he may still be subject to the duty to avoid conflicts of interest and the duty not to accept benefits from third parties.

     C   True. The contract may be avoided at the option of the company.

16   A   Anna is not liable because she is not guilty of any breach of duty. She might be negligent in failing to spot the transaction. Directors in breach are jointly and severally liable.

17   D   Any such provision to exclude a director from or to indemnify them against liability for breach of duty or negligence is void.

18   B   No. Civil liability only arises when a company is being wound up. Criminal liability exists regardless of whether the company is solvent or not.

       C   Yes. The standard of care is that of a reasonably diligent person, but a director is also judged by reference to their own skill, knowledge and experience. Wrongful trading is only relevant in liquidation.

19   B   No. A disqualification order (of up to 15 years) may be made in the discretion of the court.

       D   No. The court would also need to be satisfied that Elizabeth is unfit to be concerned in the management of a company (the court may take into account her conduct as a director of Big Beans Ltd) in order for a disqualification to be mandatory.

20   B   False. Only a member, or members, holding at least 15% of the class of shares in question may apply.

       C   True. In fact, holders of at least 5% of the company's paid up capital with voting rights can requisition a meeting.

21   B   No. It is not necessary to show this.

       D   No. Such authorisation or ratification by the company will be binding and a derivative action will not be appropriate.

22   A   True.

       D   False, although relief is considerably less likely to be given in the absence of any such breach.

23   B   All of these are possible orders. However, the most common relief granted is an order for the majority to purchase the minority's shares, valued on the basis of the shares' worth before they were diminished by the conduct of the controlling shareholders.

24   A   Yes.

       D   No. This is a remedy of last resort. In this case there is clearly an alternative to liquidation (buying out his shares).

25   C   The articles may require a higher percentage up to 95%.

26   C   Unless all members entitled to attend and vote agree to a shorter period.

27   A   True.

       D   False. A public limited company must pass resolutions in general meeting.

28   D   Only an ordinary resolution is required, but with special notice of 28 days.

29   B   No. A written resolution cannot be used in order to remove a director or auditor from office.

       C   Yes. For example, model articles provide for the removal of bankrupt directors.   SAMPLE PAPER

30   A   Yes. A director must act in good faith for the benefit of the company and must also avoid any conflict of interest.

       C   Yes. Exploiting such an opportunity constitutes a breach of duty, regardless of whether the company could actually take advantage of the opportunity itself.   SAMPLE PAPER

31   C   These facts are most likely to amount to a breach of the duty of care owed by a director, particularly since he is a managing director.   SAMPLE PAPER

32   B   False. A director is not an agent of the shareholders and is not liable to act as instructed by them.

       D   False. A director owes a duty to exercise independent judgement. Such an agreement would constitute a breach of this duty. He may, however, act in accordance with an agreement duly entered into by the company restricting the future exercise of discretion by its directors or in any way authorised by the company's constitution.   SAMPLE PAPER

33   C   A company director may be removed by the passing of an ordinary resolution with special notice. The other options require the passing of a special resolution.   SAMPLE PAPER

34   A   Relief for unfairly prejudicial conduct applies to public and private companies where the company's affairs are being, or have been, conducted in a manner that is unfairly prejudicial to the interests of members generally or some part of its members.   SAMPLE PAPER

Chapter 7: Companies: finance

1   D   Ordinary shareholders are entitled to dividends if and when they are declared by the directors, but they cannot compel the directors or the company to pay them a dividend. Preference shareholders are (typically) entitled to receive a dividend at a specified rate before any other dividend is paid or declared, but they do not have the right to compel payment of a dividend.

2   C   Both groups of shareholders have the same rights and so both get their capital repaid and share equally if there is anything left over after repayment of capital. Where the articles state that the preference shareholders have a preferential right to the return of capital, that is all they receive (before payment to ordinary shareholders) with any surplus being exclusively for the ordinary shareholders.

3   B   False. In the absence of any express provision, preference shares carry the same voting rights as ordinary shares. Typically, however, preference shares are expressed not to carry voting rights (or only to carry them in specified circumstances).

     C   True.

4   A   Yes.

     C   Yes.

5   B   The members making this application to the court must not have voted for the variation.

6   C   The fact that the value of existing rights may be affected does not constitute a variation of those rights.

7   A   True.

     C   True. Any part of the share capital that is not issued is called 'unissued share capital'.

8   A   The authority can be general or specific, conditional or unconditional.

9   A   Yes. The directors of a private company with only one class of shares may allot shares of that class unless such an allotment is prohibited by the company's articles.

     C   Yes. Failure to register the allotment within two months is an offence punishable by a fine.

10 A   True.

     D   False. There is no obligation on the members to take additional shares. Indeed, they may sell their rights and obtain value for their option over those shares.

11 A   The pre-emption rights are expressed (by the Companies Act 2006) not to apply to (2), (3) and (4).

12 A   Yes. A sum equal to the premium on each share must be transferred to a share premium account.

     D   No (although a commission may be paid to someone who agrees to subscribe for or to procure subscriptions for shares in the company, in accordance with a company's articles of association).

13 B   False. This is true in respect of public companies but not private companies.

     D   False. Again, this is true only for public companies.

14 B   No. Shares in a public company cannot be paid for by an undertaking to perform work or services for the company.

     D   No. Shares in a public limited company must be paid up by at least one quarter of the nominal value when issued.

15 A   True.

     C   True.

16	B	No. Only in respect of listed shares.
	D	No. However regulations may be made (under the Companies Act 2006) by the Treasury or Secretary of State which will make it compulsory.
17	A	Yes. (A company does this by passing an ordinary resolution to that effect (and subject to any restrictions in its articles)).
	C	Yes. (A company does this by passing an ordinary resolution to that effect (and subject to any restrictions in its articles)).
18	D	A public limited company must re-register as a private company unless the court orders otherwise.
19	B	Subdivision.
20	B	False. The company's articles may, however, restrict or exclude the issue of redeemable shares
	C	True.
21	B	False. The amount of the company's issued share capital is diminished by the nominal value of the shares redeemed.
	C	True.
22	A	The forfeiture or surrender of shares in accordance with a company's articles where there is failure to pay for them may also be permitted.
23	A	True.
	D	False. The capital redemption reserve may be used for this purpose.
24	B	The company may lend to its employees for this purpose but not to directors who are not also employees.
25	C	Whether a loan is secured or unsecured, the written acknowledgement of its terms is called a debenture.
26	A	6 months.
	D	12 months.
27	B	False. The charge will also apply to future assets.
	C	True.
28	D	Both fixed charges and preferential debts rank before floating charges.
29	C	Registration can be effected by the company or any person interested in the charge.
30	D	In addition, the money secured by the void charge is immediately repayable by the company.
31	A	Yes. A floating charge is typically over a class of assets of a company present and future with which the company may continue to deal before crystallisation of the charge.
	C	Yes. A floating charge typically covers assets that change in the ordinary course of business and only fixes to those assets at the time of crystallisation. SAMPLE PAPER
32	B	No. A company may issue shares at a premium. No express authority is required in the company's articles.
	C	Yes. Shares can be issued at a premium for cash or a non-cash consideration (although there are specific rules relating to valuation of non-cash consideration for public companies). SAMPLE PAPER
33	B	Shares of a public company are transferable on a recognised stock exchange if the company is listed. SAMPLE PAPER

Chapter 8: Insolvency law: corporate and personal

1   D   The primary purpose of administration is to rescue the company as a going concern, if at all possible.

2   A   Yes. An ordinary resolution is required.

     C   Yes. A court must be satisfied of both before it can make the necessary order.

3   A   Yes. It must notify any other qualifying floating charge holder and must satisfy the court that its floating charge is enforceable.

     D   No. A qualifying floating charge holder cannot make an administration order once a company is in liquidation (or administration or administrative receivership).

4   A   7 days.

     C   11 days.

5   B   False. The period may also be extended by a prescribed majority of creditors (but only once).

     C   True.

6   A   Yes.

     C   Yes, provided that to do so would, in their judgement, help the achievement of the purposes of administration, or otherwise with the leave of the court.

7   A   Yes.

     C   Yes. Generally speaking, the administrator has all the powers of the directors in addition to some specific powers conferred by the Insolvency Act 1986.

8   B   No. During the period of administration, there can be no resolution or court order to wind up the company.

     D   No. It can only enforce the charge with the consent of either the administrator or the court.

9   A   Yes, but it must first obtain the consent of the administrator or the court, before it can instigate or continue legal proceedings against the company.

     D   No. No resolution or petition for winding up can be passed or presented during administration.

10   A   True. The court may take various actions against the administrator.

     D   False. The company continues to be the employer (and the administrator is the company's agent) but the administrator may terminate any contracts of employment as they deem fit.

11   B   A receiver is typically appointed by a creditor with a fixed charge over property owned by the company.

12   D   All of the above.

13   B   False. Preferred and secured creditors are not bound by the CVA (unless they agree otherwise).

     D   False. The normal duration of CVA is three to five years.

14   B   Provided there are two or more directors.

     C   An ordinary resolution is sufficient.

15 A   True. Liquidation proceeds as a members' voluntary liquidation only where it can be assumed that the company's debts can be paid in full (and a declaration of solvency has been made). If the liquidator concludes that that is not the case, they must call a creditors' meeting and lay before it a statement of the company's assets and liabilities.

    C   True.

16 C   If the appointments made are different, the creditors' appointment prevails. If the creditors do not make an appointment, the members' appointment stands.

17 B   No. He must also have served a written demand on the company at its registered office and the company must have failed to pay it (or to offer reasonable security for it) within 21 days.

    D   No. This is effectively presumed by his satisfying the test referred to above.

18 B   False. On the contrary, this petition is normally presented by a member and, consequently, will only be considered where the company is solvent (otherwise the member has nothing to gain from the winding up).

    C   True.

19 C   Although he may be replaced by a qualified insolvency practitioner at a later date.

20 B   No. The company's assets remain the legal property of the company, but under Lionel's control, unless the court orders them to be vested in him as liquidator.

    C   Yes.

21 A   Yes, since it was made within two years before the liquidation.

    D   No. A liquidator does not have this power, but can apply to the court for such an order to be made.

22 A   Yes. A floating charge to a connected person may be void if entered into within the two years before the liquidation (12 months in the case of an unconnected person).

    C   Yes. This would be wholly appropriate and is part of the liquidator's role to consider such matters and take action where relevant.

23 C   Accrued holiday pay is a preferential debt, payable second, after the costs of liquidation and is followed by payment of floating charges (subject to the ring-fencing provisions). Members may receive a share of any surplus in the event that the company can, in fact, satisfy all its debts.

24 B   No. These provisions only apply where the fund available for distribution is at least £10,000.

    D   No. He should receive £100, as he ranks after all other claims listed.

25 B   A majority of 75% in value of those creditors who vote (either in person or by proxy) is required.

26 D   Any of them may present a petition for bankruptcy.

27 B   No. Where debts are less than £40,000 and the debtor's estate is worth more than £4,000 and the debtor has not been made bankrupt or entered into a scheme with their creditors in the previous five years, the court is likely to refuse a bankruptcy order and order a report to be made, with a view to achieving a suitable individual voluntary arrangement (IVA) instead.

    C   Yes. These provisions (referred to above) do not apply where a creditor petitions for bankruptcy.

28 B   False. The trustee in bankruptcy, in these circumstances, declares a dividend so that each unsecured creditor receives part payment of their debt.

    C   True. He must then pay creditors with provable debts in a prescribed order.

29 A   Yes. This is an important exception to the normal rule that the bankrupt can no longer be sued or have action taken against them by their creditors.

    C   Yes. Such vesting occurs automatically and there is no need for any written contract or transfer of rights or property.

30	B	No. Tools and equipment that are necessary for use in the debtor's employment, business or vocation are specifically excluded from the sum of their estate.
	D	No. Such a sale would be void unless approved by the court, because of his status as an undischarged bankrupt.
31	B	The liquidator's remuneration and expenses are paid first. The debt to the spouse is a postponed debt. Craig would only receive payment if there were money left once all claims on the estate had been satisfied.
32	A	Yes. Rescuing the company as a going concern is the primary objective of administration.
	C	Yes. This is also an objective of administration where rescuing the company as a going concern is not practicable. SAMPLE PAPER
33	B	No. Such a situation would not necessarily result in a winding up, which is generally a drastic remedy of last resort.
	C	Yes. If the court considers that a winding up is just and equitable, it may order compulsory liquidation. SAMPLE PAPER
34	C	Only once all debts and charges have been paid, will the shareholders be entitled to a return of their capital and, if applicable, a share in any surplus assets. SAMPLE PAPER

Chapter 9: Sole traders and partnerships

1 D No formal agreement is necessary. The '& Co' after Damian does not mean that it is a company. Equal sharing of profits does not necessarily mean that it is a partnership, since the same result could be achieved in an incorporated business.

2 B False. This is true of a limited liability partnership but not an ordinary partnership.

  C True.

3 B False. They have an express agreement as to profit-sharing and so losses will be borne in the same proportions as profits are shared.

  D False. In the absence of express provision to the contrary, partners must agree unanimously on the appointment of a new partner.

4 A True.

  D False.

5 B A partner is required to avoid conflicts of interest without full disclosure to the other partners. If the other partners know of the conflict and do not object, then the partner may proceed. A partner must account to the partnership for all monies received in respect of it.

6 A Such an appointment is within the usual authority of a partner. The fact that Hank was given express authority to appoint Jane does not detract from his implied authority to appoint. The authority was not to appoint one and no more.

7 D The Partnership Act 1890 provides that even without authority, a partner's usual acts for the partnership business are binding, unless the third party knows that they have no authority or does not know or believe them to be a partner.

8 D There is nothing to suggest that Farmer Giles is aware that Mark was acting without authority or believed him not to be a partner. Partners' acts in the usual course of business bind the firm and the partners, unless the third party knows that the partner does not have authority or does not know or believe him to be a partner.

9 B A new partner is only liable for debts incurred after they became a partner unless they agree otherwise.

10 B False. This is usually expressly provided for in a partnership agreement. However, in the absence of an express provision, the Partnership Act 1890 provides that a partnership is dissolved in a number of instances, including on the death or bankruptcy of a partner.

  C True.

11 A Yes.

  C Yes. A partnership may be wound up in the same way as an unregistered company under Part V of the Insolvency Act 1986.

12 B No. This is one of the differences between an ordinary partnership and a company.

  C Yes. He can do so, but the other person does not thereby become a partner.

13 B False. A partner can assign their interest (subject to any express provision to the contrary) but the assignee does not become a partner as a result.

  C True.

14 A True. In this respect it is like a registered company.

  D False. The liability of every LLP member is limited.

15 B No. Members are taxed as individuals on the partnership's profits.

  C Yes.

16	B	No. They may be able to use this name as a business name, but the name of an LLP must end with the words 'limited liability partnership' or the abbreviation 'LLP'.
	D	No. An LLP will normally have one but it is not essential.
17	B	No. They must submit an incorporation document in the prescribed format.
	C	Yes.
18	B	As with an ordinary partnership, there is no implied entitlement to remuneration.
19	B	False. The Limited Liability Partnership Act 2000 provides that every member is an agent of the limited liability partnership only.
	D	False. Where he acts without authority, he will still bind the LLP unless the third party knows that he does not have authority or does not know or believe him to be a member of the LLP.
20	A	They are all applicable to LLPs.
21	C	
22	B	No. In the absence of an express provision, the Partnership Act 1890 provides for the right to share in profits and losses equally.
	C	Yes. There is an implied right of access to all partnership books and accounts. SAMPLE PAPER
23	B	No, one would not be sufficient. The requirement is for two or more persons to subscribe their names to the incorporation document.
	C	Yes, this is also a requirement. SAMPLE PAPER
24	B	No. There is no statutory right to remuneration.
	C	Yes. In the absence of express provision, there is an implied right to share in the profits of the LLP equally. SAMPLE PAPER
25	B	False. Licences and VAT registration are only required for certain classes and size of business and so do not apply to all sole traders.
	C	True. The main benefit of operating as a sole trader is that all business profits accrue to the trader.
26	C	Sole traders are not subject to audit and do not have to file accounts with the Registrar. They are required to report to the tax authorities as part of the sole trader's personal tax return. A sole trader's business is not legally distinct from their personal wealth – this is the main disadvantage of operating as a sole trader.

Chapter 10: Criminal law

1   B   No. The Act applies to 'workers' (which is wider than 'employees' but does not include the self-employed).

    D   No.

2   B   False. There is no requirement as to length of continuous service.

    D   False. He will, however, need to have a reasonable belief that the health and safety of an individual has been, is being, or is likely to be endangered.

3   C   While rumour and suspicion are unlikely to satisfy the need for reasonable belief, it is not necessarily the case that someone will need to produce documentary evidence.

4   C   Criminal offences and unsafe working practices are qualifying disclosures.

5   A   True.

    C   True. In all cases the worker should have a reasonable belief that the information disclosed to the regulatory body concerned is indeed true.

6   A   True.

    D   False. There is no longer a requirement for good faith, but the apparent lack of good faith may result in any compensation being reduced by up to 25%. The disclosure must be made in the public interest.

7   B   False. Nina could disclose the information to the Minister responsible for the NHS and still receive the statutory protection (even though the aim of the Act is to encourage internal disclosure in the first instance).

    C   True. A tribunal may award an amount that it considers just and equitable in all the circumstances and there is no maximum limit.

8   B   False. The 1998 Act is aimed at encouraging internal disclosure but it is not always appropriate or necessary.

    C   True.

9   A   Yes. It must be reasonable in all the circumstances and must not be made for personal gain.

    D   No. This is one option, but alternatively he may show that he had a reasonable belief that a cover-up was likely and there was no prescribed regulator or a reasonable belief that he would be victimised if he raised the matter internally or with a prescribed regulator.

10 B   No. The offence is also committed where the defendant intended to cause another person loss or to expose that person to the risk of making that loss. (This is true whichever of the three instances of fraud applies.)

    D   No. He faces the possibility of being disqualified, however, for up to 15 years as a result.

11 D   10 years' imprisonment and an unlimited fine is the maximum penalty for fraud under the Fraud Act 2006.

12 A   Yes. (Civil liability on the other hand, arises only where a company is in liquidation.)

    C   Yes.

13 B   The offence can be committed by any person who is knowingly a party to the company's business being carried on with intent to defraud creditors.

14 C   No statutory definition of 'fraudulent' is given but it seems that some positive act is needed and not just neglect. Nigel may be in breach of his director's duty to exercise reasonable care and skill however. The fact that Leo is not a director does not mean that he has no potential liability.

15	B	
16	A	Yes. Richard is guilty of encouraging another person to deal.
	D	No. It is irrelevant whether any dealing actually takes place.
17	B	No. He does not know or have reasonable cause to believe that Freya will deal.
	C	Yes. The disclosure is not made in the proper performance of their employment and so an offence is committed under the Criminal Justice Act 1993.
18	A	Yes. The information relates to particular securities and is price-sensitive, as it would be likely to have a significant effect on the price of the securities if made public.
	C	Yes, because she obtained the information from an insider, Andy, who had the information by virtue of his profession as auditor.
19	B	No, provided she can demonstrate that she would have purchased the shares in any event.
	D	No. Disclosing information in the course of employment is not an offence under the 1993 Act. Assuming he did not also encourage Karl to buy, he has committed no offence.
20	B	False. Bribery may be committed by either the recipient or the offeror of the money or favour.
	D	False. The person bribed may be in public office or in business. They must be in a position of trust or otherwise expected to perform their function or activity in good faith or impartially.
21	B	False. An offer is sufficient. It is immaterial whether the offer is accepted.
	C	True. It is likely that the managing director of a public limited company would be regarded as a person in business who is expected to perform their functions impartially and in good faith.
22	A	True. The Bribery Act 2010 replaced the offence at common law and repealed several statutes dealing with corruption.
	D	False. The maximum term of imprisonment is 10 years.
23	D	
24	A	Plus an unlimited fine. The principal offence of money laundering is punishable by 14 years' imprisonment and tipping off by two years.
25	B	No. Although he has been concerned in an arrangement suspecting that it will facilitate use of criminal property (ie, the proceeds of tax evasion), he has a defence, in that he has reported the matter to the MLRO.
	D	No. The offence of tipping off is committed when a disclosure is made to a third party that a disclosure or report has been made, where that disclosure is likely to prejudice any resulting investigation, or when a disclosure is made that an investigation is being contemplated or carried out and that disclosure is likely to prejudice the investigation.
26	B	If the client had been worried that tax might not have been paid adequately and was seeking advice in order to correct the situation, these would be privileged circumstances and provide a defence to a failure to report, under the Proceeds of Crime Act 2002.
27	A	Yes. Failure to do so would be an offence. The Proceeds of Crime Act 2002 offers protection where information rightly disclosed results in a breach of confidentiality.
	D	No. He should only report to the MLRO. He must then be aware that revealing his suspicions to any other person could constitute the offence of tipping off, if it is likely to prejudice an investigation into the company's affairs.
28	B	False. A business must appoint a MLRO.
	C	True.
29	B	False. A defendant will have a defence if they can show that their conduct was necessary for the proper exercise of any function of either an intelligence service or the armed forces when engaged on active service.
	D	False. If the commercial organisation can show that it had 'adequate procedures' in place to prevent bribery, it will not be guilty.

30	A	Yes. Disclosure of such activity would amount to a qualifying disclosure.
	C	Yes. Likewise, disclosure of endangering the health and safety of employees would amount to a qualifying disclosure. SAMPLE PAPER
31	A	True.
	C	True. Up to 10 years' imprisonment (and/or an unlimited fine) is the maximum penalty for fraudulent trading. SAMPLE PAPER
32	A	True.
	D	False. Fraudulent trading is a criminal offence and it is not sufficient to show the officer 'suspected' the company might not be able to pay its debts. SAMPLE PAPER
33	A	True. The offence is committed whether or not the offeree accepts the money or other favour.
	C	True. SAMPLE PAPER
34	A	True. It was held in *Royal Bank of Scotland v Bannerman Johnstone Maclay* 2005 that a third party can be owed a duty of care where auditors know their identity, the use to which the information would be put and that the third party intends to rely on it. Brisco LLP was aware of Wyman plc and that the company would be relying on the audited financial statements when making a takeover bid. Therefore a duty of care is owed.
	C	True. Abel Brisco is likely to be in breach of professional behaviour. By denying that he had not been notified of Wyman's reliance on the financial statements he will be lying. This is dishonest and likely to bring the profession into disrepute.
35	B	The term 'money laundering' covers any activity by which the apparent source and ownership of the proceeds of crime are changed, in such a way that the cash or other assets appear to have been obtained legitimately. Gavin has not conducted any such activity because payment of a dividend which is illegal under the Companies Act 2006 is not a criminal offence.
	C	Gavin is party to the deception of users of the financial statements who will believe the dividend was legitimate. Deception is dishonest and is likely to bring the profession into disrepute, hence he is in breach of professional behaviour.
36	B	No. Generally speaking, the need to make a report to the National Crime Agency takes precedence over considerations of client confidentiality. The Proceeds of Crime Act 2002 offers protection where information rightly disclosed under the Act results in a breach of confidentiality. Therefore the client cannot take legal action against the firm.
	D	No. Under the ICAEW Code of Ethics, where an accountant is required by law or regulations to disclose confidential information, they shall always disclose that information in compliance with relevant legal requirements. Therefore Harriet has not breached the rules on confidentiality.
37	B	Keylogging is where criminals record what the user types onto their keyboard.
38	A	True. The use of emails to obtain bank information such as this is known as phishing.
	D	False. Phishing emails are an example of fraud by representation (dishonestly making a false representation of fact or law, intending thereby to make a gain for oneself or another or to cause another party loss or expose that party to the risk of making loss.)
39	B	Accidentally spreading a virus is not an offence. The creation of ransomware and hacking are both offences, as is the unauthorised access to content stored on a computer such as a colleague's email account.

1   C   Do not confuse with a contract of service which is another name for an employment contract between an employer and an employee.

2   A   Personal service is a necessary element of a contract of service. Although a limited ability to delegate is acceptable, an absolute prohibition makes it more likely that it will be a contract of service. B, C and D are all consistent with a contract for services.

3   D   This suggests a contract for services, although it is not conclusive. A, B and C are all consistent with a contract of service.

4   B   False. Although the existence of these elements is absolutely essential in order for a contract to be held to be a contract of service rather than a contract for services, their existence does not necessarily mean that this will be the case. The application of the multiple test may still result in the arrangement being a contract for services.

    C   True. In such cases there is an absence of mutuality of obligations, which is an essential ingredient for the existence of a contract of service.

5   B   The courts apply a multiple test and all the factors, save with regard to payment of tax and delegation to some extent, suggest a contract of employment. A limited power of delegation is not inconsistent with a contract of employment.

6   C   Although most factors are consistent with a contract of service, the absence of the mutuality of obligations means that it cannot be one. If Bun the Baker were under an obligation to provide her with work and she was under an obligation to do it, then it would be a contract of employment.

7   B   No. An employee still makes social security contributions, but primary class I contributions rather than class 2 and class 4 contributions.

    C   Yes. Where their employer has dismissed them in breach of their employment contract they can bring a claim within six years of the date of their dismissal. An independent contractor cannot claim wrongful dismissal.

8   A   Yes. An employee, on the other hand, would not register for VAT separately from their employer.

    D   No. Under the Employment Rights Act 1996, only employees have the right to bring a claim for unfair dismissal.

9   A   Yes. An independent contractor, on the other hand, is directly responsible to the HM Revenue and Customs for income tax due.

    D   No. An independent contractor is still owed statutory duties by their employer under the Health and Safety at Work Act 1974, although an employee is owed a greater duty of care. Moreover, under the common law, an employer has a duty to protect their employees against reasonably foreseeable risks to their health, safety and welfare.

10 B   False. An employment contract can be created orally.

    C   True. Terms may be implied by common law or statute. For example legislation provides that all employees should have equality of terms and conditions of employment relating to pay.

11 C   Two months, in accordance with the Employment Rights Act 1996.

12 B   No. There are no criminal sanctions. Rather, the employee may apply for a declaration of rights stating what the particulars of their employment should be and the employer may be liable to pay compensation to the employee in certain circumstances.

    D   No. This will be sufficient to replace the need for a written statement.

13   A   The duty of fidelity is a common law duty owed by an employee to their employer to provide faithful service. Marmaduke is liable to be dismissed because he has acted in breach of this implied term of his employment contract and will be liable to account to Fashions First Ltd for all the secret commissions that he has received.

14   B   False. There is no such duty if the instructions would require them to do an unlawful act or expose them to danger or to do something outside their employment contract.

      D   False. Naturally most duties do cease when the employment ceases. However, the duty not to misuse confidential information may continue after that time.

15   B   No. There is no such duty on the employer implied by common law.

      C   Yes. The employer owes a duty at common law to pay reasonable remuneration. This duty is subject to any express provision, for example to pay a rate fixed by the parties, or to pay nothing during a lay-off.

16   B   No. The duty is to pay the agreed remuneration and, in the absence of express provision, to pay a reasonable amount (subject to the legal requirements concerning the minimum wage).

      C   Yes. Generally speaking, there is an implied obligation to provide work or to continue to pay wages where no work is provided. Where an employee is paid on a commission only basis (as Amran is here), the duty is to give the employee the opportunity to earn their commission.

17   A   True. However, he may do so in those cases where he has received the employee's consent.

      D   False. There is no obligation on an employer to provide a reference, but if an employer chooses to do so, they must exercise reasonable care and skill in order to ensure that the information relayed in the reference is accurate and fair.

18   D   The company and any director or other officer who consents to or is responsible for the commission of the offence may be liable to an unlimited fine and up to two years' imprisonment.

19   B   An employee who has continuous employment of between one month and 24 months is entitled to at least one week's notice.

20   D   The 1996 Act provides that an employee with continuous employment with the same or an associated employer of between 2 and 12 years is entitled to not less than one week's notice per year of service.

21   C   The Employment Rights Act 1996 provides that the minimum period of notice is not less than 12 weeks where an employee has continuous employment with the same or an associated employer of 12 years or more.

22   A   Yes.

      D   No. However, a failure to comply with a relevant procedure, including the Acas Code, may render a dismissal unfair.

23   A   True.

      D   False. The claim may be reduced by up to 25%.

24   C   A, B and D are potentially fair reasons for dismissal under the Employment Rights Act 1996 (subject to the requirement that the employer has acted reasonably in the circumstances), and require the employee to have been continuously employed for at least two years at the employee's effective date of termination.

25   C   Three months.

26   D   These circumstances would frustrate the contract. Frustration of a contract does not constitute dismissal for the purposes of unfair dismissal protection.

27   A   True, since this is an automatically unfair reason for dismissal.

      C   True.

28   A   Yes. Potentially fair reasons include that the employee's conduct is unacceptable and that the employee lacks the capability or qualification for the job which they are employed to do.

      C   Yes. It is a question of fact for the tribunal to decide on all the evidence whether the employer acted reasonably in treating the reason as sufficient grounds for dismissal.

29   D   (Assuming that the Sunshine Care Home has followed the Statutory Disciplinary and Dismissal Procedure.) It should be noted that, when making their decisions in employment cases, employment tribunals take into account the fairness of their decision in relation to the employer, as well as to the employee concerned.

30   D   The basic award is calculated by reference to an employee's age and length of service. It may be reduced on account of an employee's unreasonable behaviour and any redundancy payment will also be taken into account.

31   A   Yes.

      C   Yes.

32   C   D is also a remedy for wrongful dismissal but damages is the usual remedy that is awarded.

33   B   No. He does not have a sufficient period of continuous employment (of two years) with Hots Ltd.

      C   Yes. Wrongful dismissal is a common law action where the employer dismisses the employee in breach of contract. In the present case Oliver's employer has acted in breach of his implied duty of mutual trust and confidence.

34   C   Raita may sue for the agreed sum, ie, the equivalent of six months' salary, under the contract and will be under no duty to mitigate her loss. Continuous employment is irrelevant to an action for wrongful dismissal (B).

35   A   This is not a wrongful dismissal because Arthur has engaged in gross misconduct justifying his summary dismissal.

36   A   True.

      C   True. It is calculated in the same way as a basic award for unfair dismissal (based on an employee's age and length of service).

37   A   Yes. The requirements of Bespoke Windows Ltd for work of a particular type have ceased.

      D   No. An employee must have two years' or more continuous employment with the same or an associated employer at the relevant date, in order to be entitled to claim a statutory redundancy payment.

38   B   He should apply to the employment tribunal within six months of the relevant date of his dismissal by reason of redundancy, although the tribunal has a (rarely exercised) discretion to allow a late claim within the following six months also.

39   A   Yes. The requirements of Complete Gardens Ltd for work of a particular type have ceased.

      C   Yes. The new post, although at the same premises and for the same salary, would be perceived as being lower in status and he is not bound to accept it, on the grounds that it is not suitable alternative employment in accordance with the 1996 Act.

40   A   Yes. Employees have the right not to be unfairly dismissed.

      D   No. Employees are paid net of income tax and national insurance contributions.

SAMPLE PAPER

41   A   True. Where the worker undertakes a degree of financial risk, this is generally regarded as a factor consistent with a contract for services.

      C   True. This power of limited delegation is consistent with Andrew being an employee.

SAMPLE PAPER

42   A   Yes. Terms may be implied into a contract of employment by common law and by statute where no express provision is made.

      D   No. The prescribed particulars may provide evidence of the terms of a contract of employment but the written statement does not actually form part of that contract.
SAMPLE PAPER

43   A   True. This is a duty implied at common law and owed by employers to their employees.

      C   True. Damages is the most likely remedy.   SAMPLE PAPER

44   A   Yes. Termination of a fixed-term contract before the expiry date constitutes a dismissal.

      C   Yes. Termination with no, or insufficient, notice constitutes a dismissal.   SAMPLE PAPER

45   A   Yes. Dismissal on the grounds of membership or non-membership of a trade union or the taking part in protected industrial action is automatically unfair.

      C   Yes. Dismissal on such grounds is likely to be automatically unfair.   SAMPLE PAPER

46   A   True.

      D   False. In order to be fairly dismissed on the grounds of lack of qualification, there must be a contractual obligation to hold that qualification.   SAMPLE PAPER

47   B   False. An employee must have at least two years' continuous service in order to claim a statutory redundancy payment.

      C   True. The employee must have been dismissed, laid off or put on short-time working in order to succeed in a claim.   SAMPLE PAPER

48   B   False. The Act also applies to manual files.

      C   True.

49   A   Yes.

      C   Yes.

50   A   Homemade Cakes Ltd should also bear in mind the potential costs that it may incur as a consequence of being required to rectify its databases.

51   A   True.

      D   False. It is a public register.

52   A   True. This is one of the eight data protection principles.

      D   False. There is no such obligation on the data controller. The data subject must request information in accordance with their right of access.

53   B   No. The right to compensation only lies if the claimant can show that they have suffered damage as a result of a contravention of the Act.

      C   Yes. This is one of the rights given by the Act to protect data subjects.

54   B   No. Data held by unincorporated members' clubs are exempt from the Act and, therefore, there is no right of access to them under the Act.

      D   No. Since clubs' data are exempt from the Act, there is no such right to compensation available to Amy.

55   B   False. All data pertaining to a data subject are accessible by the data subject whatever the form in which they are held.

      D   False. The data subject can obtain both rectification and compensation.   SAMPLE PAPER

56   A   Yes. Copyright applies to music, film and art.

      D   No. Copyright is granted automatically and does not have to be applied for.

57   D   Trademarks are used to protect product names and logos.

58   C   Patents apply to inventions and products, such as machines or parts of machines.

Mock exam
guidance notes

Exam standard

The mock exam should be set at the same level represented as the 2016 sample papers on the ICAEW website.

Exam format

The mock exam should consist of 50 questions each worth 2 marks.

Style of exam questions

Each question should conform to the style used in the sample paper ie,

- Multiple Choice Question (MCQ) (1 from 4); or
- 2-part MCQ (eg, 3 × 'true or false').

There is no partial marking, so all parts of a question must be answered correctly to obtain 2 marks.

Exam coverage and balance

A mock exam should reflect the weightings in the syllabus specification grid as follows:

Syllabus area	Weighting (%)	Number of questions
1 The impact of civil law on business and professional services	35	17
2 Company and insolvency law	40	20
3 The impact of criminal law on business and professional services	10	5
4 The impact of law in the professional context	15	8
Total	100	50

A suggested format for a mock exam is as follows:

Syllabus area	Structure/format
1	17 questions covering learning outcomes a to g, eg, • 8 questions relating to contract; • 4 questions relating to agency; and • 5 questions relating to negligence and liability.
2	20 questions covering the learning outcomes a to p.
3	5 questions covering the learning outcomes a to g.
4	8 questions covering the learning outcomes a to g, eg, • 3 on information and its legal environment; and • 5 on employment law and social security law

REVIEW FORM – LAW: Question Bank

Your ratings, comments and suggestions would be appreciated on the following areas of this Question Bank

	Very useful	Useful	Not useful
Number of questions in each section	☐	☐	☐
Standard of answers	☐	☐	☐
Amount of guidance on exam technique	☐	☐	☐
Quality of marking guides	☐	☐	☐

	Excellent	Good	Adequate	Poor
Overall opinion of this Question Bank	☐	☐	☐	☐

Please return completed form to:
The Learning Team
Learning and Professional Department
ICAEW
Metropolitan House
321 Avebury Boulevard
Milton Keynes
MK9 2FZ
E learning@icaew.com

For space to add further comments please see overleaf.

REVIEW FORM (continued)

TELL US WHAT YOU THINK

Please note any further comments and suggestions/errors below.